Smart Marketing

What Big Companies Practice and You Should Learn About Marketing, Branding and Business Development

Stan Rosenzweig

TECHNICAL COLLEGE OF THE LOWCOUNTRY
LEARNING RESOURCES CENTER
POST OFFICE BOX 1288
BEAUFORT, SOUTH CAROLINA 29901-1288

Emery Publishing
Stamford, Connecticut

© 2000 Stan Rosenzweig

All rights reserved.
This book may not be duplicated in any way without the express written consent of the author, except in the form of brief excerpts or quotations for the purposes of review. The information contained herein is for the personal use of the reader and may not be incorporated in any commercial programs or other books, databases, or any other kind of software without the written consent of the publisher or author. Making copies of this book, or any portion of it, for any purpose other than your own, is a violation of United States copyright laws.

PRINTED IN THE UNITED STATES OF AMERICA

ISBN 1-58652-002-4

Smart Marketing: LCCN: 00-106135

    Publisher's Cataloging-in-Publication

    Rosenzweig, Stan.
      Smart Marketing : what big companies practice and you should learn about marketing, branding, and business development / Stan Rosenzweig. – 1st ed.
    p. cm.

    ISBN 1-58652-002-4

Books by Stan Rosenzweig

Smart Selling How You Can Turn Ordinary Selling Into Extraordinary Income. Twenty lessons that have helped thousands to earn millions.

Smart Marketing What Big Companies Practice And You Should Learn About Marketing, Branding And Business Development.

Smart Telemarketing How You Can Turn Ordinary Telemarketing Into Extraordinary Income.

Smart Sales Management How You Can Use The Powerful Lessons Of Others To Help You To Build And Lead A Winning Sales And Management Team.

Smart Thinking How To Use Your Own Life Experiences To Reach Greater Success. Chicken soup may be good, but front line sales experience is better.

Sailing For Non-Sailors What Every Guest Should Know Before Stepping Aboard.

Hotel Telecommunications Opportunities Through Deregulation.

TABLE OF CONTENTS

LESSON ONE ....
— Introduction
Marketing without tears. What marketing is, and how to do it.

LESSON TWO ....
— Life's Lessons in Advertising
Three conclusions drawn from real life examples. What an interview with the legendary real estate builder Sam Lefrak taught me.

LESSON THREE ....
— More Lessons in Advertising
How to apply firm cost-benefit rules to your media choices. Exploring concepts to get the most bang for your bucks.

LESSON FOUR ....
— How to Get Great Press Coverage
Not all print media is costly. Here's how to get your name out there more often. Step-by-step guide to getting your message published over and over again...and for free.

LESSON FIVE ....
— The Power of Branding
Branding isn't a luxury for big budget companies. It's a necessity for small cost-conscious ones who hope to grow. Here's how to boost your sales numbers with better branding.

LESSON SIX ....
— Hair-Raising Brands
A branding strategy alone won't guarantee you'll remain the market leader, but without it you'll never get there. Ways to create your brand and then keep it strong in the hearts and minds of your customers.

LESSON SEVEN ....
- Jordan, Tiger, Hot Dogs & You
There's a lot more to pricing than figuring percentages over cost. The key marketing concepts that will shape your marketing strategies and multiply your margins.

LESSON EIGHT ....
— Advertising Specialties That Work
There's a right way, and a wrong way to distribute trinkets. How to turn specialty gifts from cheap trinkets to grand image builders.

Smart Marketing

LESSON NINE ....
— Newsletters Can Restart Marketing Engines
This low-cost, easy-to-implement program provides better than average ROI. A ten point plan for newsletter marketing success.

LESSON TEN ....
— Your Stationery Should Sell Too
Your wastebasket is filled with bad business stationery. Learn from this. Eight tips for making a better printed impression.

LESSON ELEVEN ....
— The Real Value of Market Research
Look closely at your market, and rewards will follow. Four keys from a Yale Ph.D. on how to get the answers you need.

LESSON TWELVE ....
— Garbage In-Garbage Out
If you want meaningful data, ask the right questions. Potato growers get it right. Our Department of Commerce doesn't.

LESSON THIRTEEN ....
— Talk Is Cheap
Horror stories about stuff that doesn't work, and how the market reacts. Does your product measure up to what you promise? Does it really matter?

LESSON FOURTEEN ....
— The Devil's in the Details
How I beat an extradition order and a fraud rap in Kentucky. It's amazing how a little mistake in a database can gum up your whole marketing day.

LESSON FIFTEEN ....
— Pricing as Marketing
How does creative pricing improve sales? Higher prices aren't always the most profitable.

LESSON SIXTEEN ....
— Getting the Job Done Through People...and Printing
How to use collateral materials and people wisely. Of all the means available to take your products to market, here are a few practical tips before you pay the printer.

Table of Contents

LESSON SEVENTEEN ....
– Charging for Support
What part of your service is proprietary and worth more? Unbundling services can improve your year end bottom line. Here's how.

LESSON EIGHTEEN ....
– Adding Value to Commodities
Don't fool yourself into believing that you add value. How to separate the real value from the commodity.

LESSON NINETEEN ....
– Greater Wealth Through Smart Positioning
Redefine your market by developing new products and services to sell to your existing customer base. Four steps to reposition your way to success and a three step plan to roll it out.

LESSON TWENTY ....
– Seven Creative Ways to Reach Your Marketing Objectives Without Paying an Arm and a Leg
These seven promotions are easy to accomplish, are low in cost, and just as important, they are charitable. They improve your brand image in the community and increase sales. 1. Give away the store. 2. Sponsor a school essay contest. 3. Newsletter delights. 4. Linkage. 5. The greater glory promotion. 6. The altruistic seminar. 7. The turkey trot.

LESSON TWENTY-ONE ....
– Marketing Is ...
The point to all of this marketing talk. The times they are a changing. How to keep up...or better yet, how to get ahead of the curve.

LESSON ONE

Introduction

Marketing without tears. What marketing is, and how to do it.

*J*ust what I needed, I groaned, as I listened to another hare-brained, $60,000 marketing proposal from some kid who never had to make a payroll in his life. I was committed to throwing him out of my office when he said, "Stop! Just tell me what you think that marketing should do for you. If you know what you want, I can deliver."

That got my attention, so I released my grip on the seat of his pants and the back of his neck and said, "Give me six good ideas that take very little of my time, cost even less of my money and will earn me more money than they cost me even from the first day."

Needless to say, the kid was history and his mutterings of "impossible", "unreasonable", and "jerk" could be heard as he faded away down the hallway. In retrospect, the kid wasn't as dumb as he looked, because an hour later he was on the phone asking me if I really thought that it was possible to come up with a half dozen really good ideas that would truly be cost effective right from the start. If I could, he wanted to help me implement them and maybe port a few of them from my hectic business to his own sagging marketing company.

Sure, I told him and we set about to do just that. What we came up with was more than six ways to improve our marketing with little or no money down. We developed a philosophy for generating community presence, tons of good will, a sense of integrity and the image of a can-do company. It's a philosophy that anyone in business can adopt and it may actually make going to work a lot more fun.

First of all, let's define what marketing is and isn't. It is not sales. I wish I had a nickel for how many guys come knocking on my door saying they're in marketing. Marketing is not selling.

Marketing is something that the better you do, the easier it is to sell.

The UPS guys know about marketing. Is anybody beating down your door from UPS asking for an order? No. They have marketed so well that we beat down their door and invite them over.

In our own computer-related business there are sales companies and marketing companies. Those of us in the business technology arena, for the most part, are in sales. When it's Miller time we swap war stories about how Lotus 1-2-3, WordPerfect, and Paradox were great products compared with Microsoft Office, which, as you well know, still owns the market.

We argue 'til the cows come home about who's got the fastest, snappiest, user interface, or who has written the most elegant lines of code; but without great marketing the greatest choices of professionals lie in dusty, unopened cartons in the backs of low-rent warehouses.

Those at the Mom and Pop end of the selling spectrum,

Introduction

who can't afford high priced marketing wars, often daydream about that one great promotion that will have customers lined up and down the block and around the corner. But it is hard to think of spending money for marketing when you have over sold your regional distributor credit limit and your check book balance will just about cover this afternoon's UPS C.O.D. delivery.

If that's your situation (even if it isn't now, I'll bet, you've been there once or twice in your lifetime), there are a half dozen things that I have done recently, or have talked one of my gullible friends into doing, that can really turn your business around. You know marketing works and you ought to be doing it. These schemes may appear hare-brained to some, but they all work. At least, if the results are less than you hoped, they will not have cost you much.

In this training program, I have collected numerous successful marketing strategies, programs and techniques that have been very well received in dozens of successful magazine columns. Many readers, people like you, have reported that these ideas have helped them reach new financial heights without having to mortgage the farm in order to bring in high-priced Madison Avenue teams.

These columns were designed for owners and managers of small and medium-sized service businesses, but they work well in almost any enterprise. This is not an MBA course. It is a no-nonsense guide to increasing your sales in the cheapest, most straightforward and least exhausting manner. What else could you ask for?

So, dig in and start using these ideas today. Next month, drop me a note and let me know how this book helped you increase earnings and improve your business.

LESSON TWO

Life's Lessons in Advertising
. . . . . .

Three conclusions drawn from real life examples. What an interview with the legendary real estate builder Sam Lefrak taught me.

G ood advertising is always a judgment call. There's a lot you can learn about advertising from life. Take skiing, for instance. My friend Robbie Stillerman told me that she would ski better if she weren't so fearful of falling down and breaking her assets.

Robbie owns an art design studio and her assets (good looks and great sales abilities aside) are her artist's hands. Clearly, Robbie's fear is tied to her ability to sustain her occupation.

Robbie felt that fear was an unreasonable handicap to overcome. I, on the other hand, being totally modern in outlook, don't see someone with fear, necessarily, as being handicapped, since the word "handicap", today, is politically and socially incorrect. Perhaps we should think of Robbie as being courageously challenged...but not so unreasonably so, if you think about it.

Smart Marketing

"If you are unsure of yourself on skis, can't easily stop when you want to, can't change directions as local conditions require and can't moderate your speed once you commit down a path, your fear is not unreasonable," I suggested. "That fear is genetically-programmed self-preservation and shows, at least, good judgment, which seems to be in critical short supply these days."

All these new "yes I can" books, tapes, seminars and such, are not always wise, either. Good judgment, to me, is not simply pumping yourself up with positive mental platitudes and other intellectual Prozac, but taking honest inventory of your strengths and weaknesses and then focusing your energies into exploiting your best strengths without wasting your time in areas where you just can't cut it. Knowing when NOT to do something is a positive attribute, too.

I have seen people past the age of 70 take up skiing for the first time. But what if you have osteoporosis? In that case, skiing is still learnable after 70, but how wise is it for good long-term health? If I were taller, and younger and thinner, I could train to play for the NBA. They say that only two out of three ain't bad, but I have to face facts: I can control only one out of three on a good day.

In one recent week, I was pitched to by two different advertising agencies for the same project. I'd like to share several advertising conclusions arrived at from those two meetings that I think will be useful in the context of Robbie's ski lesson and my basketball aspirations.

Advertising Conclusion Number One:
Before you spend dollar one on any kind of advertising, write down what special value you bring to the marketplace and which of your strengths have the greatest market potential.

Lesson 2... Life's Lessons in Advertising

This will re-focus you on what is important, what you need to project and who you want to impress.

In our own companies, our core focus has always been:

1. to substantially reduce operating costs of larger corporations, very quickly, using both technology and non-technology solutions, and
2. to increase profitability by improving our clients' marketing and sales strategies.

Even I can sometimes stray from what we do best and I can get sidetracked on less profitable projects. A few years ago, I tried to emulate friend and fellow columnist Ross Murphy who once said that he never passed up an opportunity to sell a PC...even to a waitress at the local restaurant.

Well, it worked for Ross, so I decided that we might add to our volume by selling PCs. I advertised a low-cost PC for single unit retail sales and promptly lost a bundle in advertising money and in lost time that would have been more productive elsewhere. My sourcing is top notch, but low volume, low margin is just too consuming of valuable time resources for us to make it pay. Now I try to focus on our best strengths instead of trying to be all things to all people.

Advertising Conclusion Number Two:
It is imperative that you write down what you consider to be the marketing objectives of your advertising effort.

Then, choose a medium, or media, that you can afford to run with until your desired results are realized.

Look at Coke, Pepsi, AT&T, MCI Worldcom, FedEx, UPS, all the auto companies, all the airlines, Microsoft, and any current hot "dot com" company that went public in the

Smart Marketing

last year, or so: these are all heavy, heavy hitters who can afford to spend more on advertising than most of us will ever see. If it takes an extra year for a new brand to become successful, what do they care?

Clearly, these companies and big spenders of other people's money are convinced that the high-dollar cost of advertising produces results... and in many cases, it does. But does this mean that you can emulate them and bootstrap yourself up to their levels?

Maybe. The facts are, however, that mass media advertising such as radio, television, or newspapers usually cannot be counted on to produce large volumes of leads and quick results. Most successful campaigns require substantial resources, substantial stamina and substantial patience before results can even be judged.

For advertising purposes, think of businesses like shirt sizes: small, medium and large. You can pick your own numbers, but I break them down roughly into these three size categories according to annual sales dollars:

- under a million,
- one to twenty million and
- more than twenty million.

Each size needs to approach advertising from a somewhat different budgetary perspective. While the over ten million crowd is by no means one single market segment, they all share the financial ability to stay the course regardless of the lack of immediate measurable impact on sales.

If you're one of these larger companies, you can map out a strategy that calls for a protracted siege in an effort to win the hearts and minds of your identified prospective market.

Basing your program on the results of strategy number one,

Lesson 2... Life's Lessons in Advertising

you will need to establish a concept and a saturation schedule. Print advertising and radio often can take six months to a year before your audience starts to take notice. Patience and fortitude will be your partners for a long time before dividends start to roll in.

The under one million crowd doesn't have the luxury of

long-term media purchasing and, in many cases, neither do those in the under ten million category.

If you haven't broken through that ten million plateau, you really know what cash flow is all about and you, no doubt, are more interested in lead generation to keep your sales force working and profitable than you are in making your logo into a household word.

In that case, face the economic facts. You're probably better off skipping mass media, opting, instead, for the tried and true targeted direct mail, telemarketing and just plain cold canvassing. You may not reach as many people, dollar for dollar, but you'll most likely reach your objective of more qualified prospects.

Smart Marketing

Speaking of mail, there are many new companies now that provide very targeted email lists, but these are opt-in addresses of individuals who actually want to read what you have to say (They change regularly. You can find the latest ones at **www.salestipwebsite.com**).

Advertising Conclusion Number 3:
If it doesn't feel like it's going to work for you, don't do it.

You're probably right that it probably will cost you a hard-earned bundle and still won't work.

Building a business is based on your ability to make prudent choices from less than prudent alternatives. So, never risk hard-earned profits on wild speculation unless, of course, it's other people's money...which reminds me of a story.

Back in 1980, my partner took me to see a college classmate of his by the name of Richard Lefrak. Richard introduced us to his famous father Sam Lefrak, the man who conceived and built Lefrak City, low-cost housing to fulfill the American dream for returning WWII vets.

Sam was involved with his latest project, adding landfill to the crowded southern tip of Manhattan Island to create space

Lesson 2... Life's Lessons in Advertising

for new construction. Since this was new land, so to speak, Sam thought that it wouldn't come under the existing franchise of New York Telephone (which, in 1980, had exclusive monopoly rights to provide local telephone service to all of New York City) and that Sam could file to become the local telephone exchange carrier for this tiny parcel.

See, Sam knew he would never get taller or younger, so the NBA was out for him, too. But Sam played to his strengths. He knew he would never be too old to build something and he knew how to bring all the right partners to the table for yet another mega-deal.

I, on the other hand, was still young and unfocused enough to think I could go one on one with the likes of both Michael Jordan and Sam Lefrak and I wanted very much to become Sam's telephone company.

"SO," SAM ASKED ME, "HOW MUCH DO YOU THINK THIS TELEPHONE COMPANY WILL COST AND HOW DO YOU PLAN TO RAISE THE MONEY?"

I GASPED IN DISBELIEF. "MONEY?" I ASKED. "WHY YOU'RE SAM LEFRAK. YOU HAVE THE MONEY."

That was the day in 1980, in his memorabilia-laden office high above modest Queens Boulevard in Queens, New York, that Sam Lefrak taught me about judgment, risk management and prudent choices, all at once.

"LET ME TELL YOU SOMETHING, YOUNG FELLOW," HE SAID. "I NEVER USE MY OWN MONEY. THAT'S WHY THEY HAVE OPM."

Sam wouldn't. I couldn't. So, we didn't; but the lesson lingers on.

Just think of it. If John Merriweather, founder of Long

SMART MARKETING

Term Capital, had been in that office with me, he might have learned enough from cagey old Sam to have second thoughts about including his own millions (along with everyone else's billions), to leverage himself and his Nobel Laureate partners out of the poor house.

In summary, if you want to get the most from your advertising dollar: firstly, identify in writing what value you provide and how you want to portray yourself to your market; secondly, establish a set of objectives and a budget to meet them; and thirdly, trust your instincts and, like Sam Lefrak, don't blow your hard earned profits on somebody else's instincts. After all, you know your own business best and never forget, it's real money at risk.

LESSON THREE

More Lessons in Advertising
. . . . . .

How to apply firm cost-benefit rules to your media choices. Exploring concepts to get the most bang for your bucks.

Can you remember three important concepts we discussed in the last lesson that will help you apportion your advertising dollars for maximum effect?

Great! I always knew that you were paying attention. Now let's move on to the next level and use those concepts to structure a winning ad campaign for the rest of this fiscal year. What? You still can't make cost effective judgments that will provide the biggest return for your limited advertising budget? Fear not. We'll do it together.

Concept #1, if you recall, is to set down in writing those special talents, we call it value, that sets you apart from the herd.

Then decide on the image you want to project and the audience you want to impress.

Smart Marketing

Do you think that you deliver faster, like Pizza Hut? Are you capable of setting new price performance standards, like www.priceline.com? Do you see yourself as a creative problem solver, like Judge Judy? These may be value points to stress. Then again, maybe not.

Before you set yourself up with a nice new image, better look at how well these images stand the tests of time...and quality.

Back when Tandy/Radio Shack wanted to take over the computer world and actually had the resources to do it, they decided that ego, not research, would forge the logo on all their machines. They choose their initials for their model TRS-80, which everyone immediately began calling the "trash-80". The rest is history.

Compaq had the right idea and, latching on to the PC compatible standard, blasted past market-leader IBM to become the world's most popular computer in a growing market. CEO Eckart Feiffer built added value through the reselling channel and made his stockholders rich. Unfortunately, Eckert didn't notice that another competitor had an even better value model. Michael Dell learned early that the internet could create a direct one to one relationship with customers, allowing Dell to do to Compaq what Compaq did to IBM... which forced Eckert out of his CEO job. That's what happens to the best of breed when they don't keep updating the value that sets them apart from the herd.

Remember Pizza Hut, a once proud and growing food franchise? It had to rescind its "20 minutes or it's free" offer. Why? Because they couldn't and it wasn't. They ended up with red pizza sauce on their face and a very empty cash drawer. Former O.J. defense attorney Johnnie Cochran learned, too late, that his 20 minutes of fame ended way too soon (for him), for not leveraging his brand quickly and building on the well known, but fleeting, brand value.

Lesson 3... More Lessons in Advertising

Judge Judy, too, lost her quickly-amassed popularity. What can you expect from our fickle constituency who alternately champions the likes of Oprah, Regis, Martha Stewart and Jerry Springer? Never lose sight of the fact that the people who choose and then discard even Senators and Presidents this way are the very same people we all hope to sell stuff to.

Thus, deciding on what image to project and finding one that has lasting power requires more than mere intellectual thought. It requires research. Specifically, it requires marketing research.

Marketing research is how beer companies like Budweiser learn that taste doesn't sell as much as "party-hardy". It's how Bill Clinton knew what to promise us in order for him not only to get elected President, but to keep him there under the most difficult of circumstances. It's how phone companies, like AT&T, MCI, and all those 10-10-XXX guys learned, that they don't need to tell us the actual hidden charges included with their calls, so long as they keep telling us they are cheaper.

You see, with good research, it's often easier to tell what your audience wants or needs and how you might best portray yourself to win them over. Moreover, it helps you to define where your most profitable market is.

That brings us to concept #2 from the last lesson. After determining what value you want to bring to the marketplace and what image you want to project, setting down the marketing objectives of your advertising effort and choosing the media to meet your objectives become most critical to your program's success.

In a prior issue of *Investors Business Daily* (a good name to drop, by the way, if you want to one-up your *Wall Street Journal*-reading golf buddies), it was reported that ADP once determined that it could increase net earnings by 20%, if it

SMART MARKETING ——

could increase the retention level of its existing customer base by only 5%.

The company determined that it doesn't even make money from its clients until after six to nine months, according to the report, after which time an existing client becomes much more valuable than a new one. Thus, ADP learned that a significant portion of its advertising budget needed to be channeled into focus groups to keep clients an average of eight years.

By the way, in that same issue of *Investors Business Daily*, there was a guest editorial by a Mr. Kent Jeffreys about federal spending that is a perfect parallel to our discussion of how and when to spend money on advertising.

Mr. Jeffreys, in making a case against the Environmental Protection Agency, used Harvard Center for Risk Analysis statistics to relate the cost-benefit performance of some federal agencies. The thesis was that there is a finite amount of resources available to save lives, so we might as well face facts and put our money where it will do the most good (assuming, of course, that you agree that saving lives is good and is what money should be spent on in the first place).

In the Harvard Center comparison, the median cost per life-year saved by the FAA was estimated at $23,000; the National Highway Traffic Safety Commission was $78,000; OSHA was $88,000; and the EPA was $7,629,000. That's more than 331 times what the FAA needs to provide an equivalent benefit.

The conclusion drawn was that some agencies could do a lot more to improve our lives than others who sap off vital tax proceeds and, by applying cost-benefit analysis to federal agencies, we could save an additional 600,000 life-years, each year, for the same money. Think of all the Strom Thurmans's this could add to the population.

Of course, the additional cost of adding more Social Security and Medicare recipients were not counted in the figures,

Lesson 3... More Lessons in Advertising

but, still, this is a classic case of the need for our concept #2, setting down the objectives and choosing the most effective media to meet them. In this case, it is graphically clear that some programs provide a much bigger bang for the buck than others.

Is your main objective to increase market share? Do you want to increase total sales volume at any cost? How about increasing bottom line profits? Or, like the folks at ADP, are you interested in focusing on improving good will and your customer-retention statistics?

Are you marketing to any and all businesses, large and small, who will respond if you prepare your ad copy suitable for placement in newspapers, business journals, or the local Chamber of Commerce newsletter?

On the other hand, do you serve a narrow vertical niche that would not be reached effectively through these media? Or, as we discussed in the previous lesson, do you not have the kind of budget that can sustain a long-term, repetitive media buy? Must you set a modest agenda that only calls for reaching local targets of opportunity?

These questions go to the heart of the matter and your answers will enable you to tailor your advertising either through mass distribution print media, or, simply, through well-prepared, but highly-targeted, direct mail or phone marketing.

Regardless of the path you decide to take, unless someone in your outfit studied commercial art, you must retain an outside graphics artist to design your print materials, or whatever you decide to do will fail.

And that brings us to the third point of the last lesson: **If it doesn't feel like it's going to work for you, don't do it.** Regarding your home grown artwork, this is tough. It's hard to turn your back on something that you created and has become a part of you.

For some unknown reason, most of us do not seem to be

Smart Marketing

able to view the advertising material we generate in-house with the same critical eye that we use to judge materials we receive from the outside world.

Whenever we try to get our middle-schooler at home to part with her dozens of drawings, paintings, clay figures, penmanship homework (Did I say dozens? I must have meant hundreds.), we really understand the artistic torment of letting go.

I'm no different. Ever since we bought our first color printer at home, I've become entranced with the notion that I can produce high-quality, professional collateral materials. Fact is, though, I can't...and neither can you. We're professionals in the things we do and, unfortunately, commercial art is not one of them.

(Even worse, what about the software program you developed that nobody wants, or the Amiga platform that you still think will overtake Windows someday? Be fair, but be honest with yourself. If it isn't going to improve your business, dump it.)

Instead, do this. Determine what you should concentrate on selling, who you think you should be selling to, the best media to use within your budget and where you can hire a

Lesson 3... More Lessons in Advertising

professional artist. But, with common sense and professional assistance, you will have created a successful advertising campaign based on thoughtfulness, hard work and the kind of strong cost-benefit analysis that would make every one of those thousands of George Burns's tip their smelly, chewed-up cigars in approval.

LESSON FOUR

How to Get Great Press Coverage
. . . . . .

Not all print media is costly. Here's how to get your name out there more often. Step-by-step guide to getting your message published over and over again...and for free.

Here's how you can get your press releases printed. There is nothing complicated about getting good press coverage. All you need is a story that:

1. Is interesting to the publication's readers,
2. conforms to the style of the publication, and
3. reaches the right editor.

Of course, if you are writing press releases for IBM, or Microsoft, just about anything you say will meet these criteria. For the rest of us, however, a more thoughtful and targeted approach is required. I didn't say it would be easy. I just said it isn't complicated. Let's review the fundamentals of how to get published, and then look at an actual success story.

Regarding item one, the best way to develop a story that is interesting to people, other than members of your immediate family, starts with a good plan. Just as with any other important business activity, you must PLAN your press campaign around something you know about and are successful at.

Examples of local news of interest to business readers in your community may include:

- How a prominent local firm was able to expand, add more jobs and increase the local tax rolls, because you did something; or
- How a school was able to turn out a whole class of wunderkinder with assembly-line regularity as the result of your new school training program.

Examples of printable articles for trade magazine readers (like those in your vertical) include:

- How one industry leader (your customer) is getting the jump on everyone else through new innovations developed by you.
- Advance word about something bad that is going to happen to an industry, or vertical market and your just-in-the-nick-of-time solution for avoiding catastrophe.

Secondly, conforming to the style of the publication is just as important as creating reader interest. I have asked numerous editors what they look for in a story. They all say about the same thing, "Read our publication". That's good advice. I have been reading the business sections of our local city news-

Lesson 4... How to Get Great Press Coverage

paper and I have found, as you will find, that there are three ingredients to business news articles:

- They are often about big companies, or important events.
- They often have sub-plots, or secondary issues, for interest.
- They have some sort of impact on the economy - local or national.

Here is a successful press campaign that ran and how we did it. We targeted the press releases to three publications: The local city newspaper mentioned above, the regional county business news tabloid and our Chamber of Commerce newsletter.

When I speak to business owners and managers about getting press coverage, for some reason I get the impression that they don't regard publication editors as plain working folk like the rest of us. Instead, many of you act like you were back in high school about to hand in your first essay of the new school term. Isn't that ridiculous?

Well, maybe it isn't so ridiculous, after all. Consider the parallels between that new term's high school teacher you haven't gotten to know yet and a nameless, faceless editor you never even thought of getting to know. Ah, yes, the fear of the unknown.

When you're trying to sell a new account, do you let the fear of the unknown stop you? No. Do you send out an impersonal form letter and expect a signed contract by return mail? Of course not. Do you make every effort to get to know the key decision-maker, writing, faxing, calling, suggesting lunch? You do. Then why not treat editors the same way? These folks are just people, too, aren't they? If you are to meet the third criterion mentioned, reaching the right editor, you must do more than get a name. You must get an editor interested in your story.

SMART MARKETING

In our own campaign, we followed the three criteria noted at the top of this column. By doing so, we scored three out of three for published results. That is, we sent press releases to each of the three publications we had targeted and, happily, all three printed them. Their needs were served, our needs were served and the reading public was served, too. That's what I call a win-win-win. Now, the very simple secret to that success.

Because we are not IBM, or Microsoft, we felt compelled to send more than generic press releases. After all, we weren't trying to shotgun all of North America, just reach three publications. So we customized each release to conform to the style of each publication.

The story had to do with the "BUY LOCALLY" campaign that we had started, through our local Chamber of Commerce, to get major companies in our area to source locally for goods and services that are in ample local supply.

Because my research indicated that the biggest publication on our list preferred big name companies, secondary themes (or sub-plots) and economic consequences, we rolled out the program with a release that had all three. We announced the formation of a new Chamber of Commerce committee that would work to improve the economy by getting firms to source locally and had already signed a big name Fortune 100 company that supported our work. We noted that six other big name firms were about to sign, as well.

OK, so we have a good story, the first requirement, and we customized each press release to a corresponding publication, the second requirement. To complete the three-point process, I called the editors of each publication. Briefly, I explained what we were doing and what we had accomplished in so short a time. Then came the most important part.

I asked each editor for help in preparing the press re-

Lesson 4... How to Get Great Press Coverage

lease that would get published in each publication. What did they think of the story? What could I do to improve it? What kind of format, or deadline, etc., did they want me to consider before I started to write?

Not surprisingly (to me, anyway), the editors were supportive, helpful and interested. They helped me to target to their individual needs. The most important of the three, the business editor of the daily, told me I didn't need to follow the typical "press release" format. I could just write a letter, or memo, with all of the details and a staff reporter would write the story – Great!

This is similar to the point in Lesson 14 of a previous book, *Smart Selling*, where we wrote a direct marketing piece in memo format which is different from ordinary letters and, hence, got more reader notice and response.

I have found, in past attempts, that formal press releases from relative unknowns tend to get lost in the impersonal deluge of press releases that publications receive every month. On the other hand, letters, or other personally addressed correspondence, are much more likely to be considered.

I took each editor's advice, made the necessary adjustments to my draft press release and got all three published. Enough said? Try it!

LESSON FIVE

The Power of Branding

Branding isn't a luxury for big budget companies. It's a necessity for small cost-conscious ones who hope to grow. Here's how to boost your sales numbers with better branding.

This lesson is designed to cure your selling blues by reviewing the single most important marketing principle of all...yet, amazingly, one which most small companies neglect almost entirely.

This is not a quick shot in the arm, mind you. You can't apply this principle on Tuesday and expect a huge order on Friday. But it WILL bring you great success. It is a principle that is so well respected in professional marketing circles that no successful business operates without it and (from a customer's perspective) you can hardly make a buying choice in your own business or personal life without being swayed by its effects.

If you can't figure it out, here's a hint in the form of a riddle that my friend Steve Olsen called me with from California:

Smart Marketing

Steve asked me, "What's the difference between a Hoover and a Harley?"

"I dunno." I said. "What possibly could be the difference between a Hoover and a Harley?"

"The position of the dirtbag."

Not bad, Steve. A dirty joke without the smut.

What makes this joke funny, however, is more than a play on the word dirtbag, which isn't funny by itself. It is also that we already know the two products. We know that Hoover is one of many brand names of vacuum cleaners. More importantly, we know Harley as one of the world's truly romantic brand names synonymous not just with road bikes but with the big, bad, mother of all road bikes.

There are many other motorcycle companies, but they don't have the same brand image that Harley Davidson has. This joke just wouldn't work if we asked the difference between a Hoover and a Honda. So, the key to this joke, as with most marketing success, is the effectiveness of brand identification.

Consider that, for the most part, a shoe is just a shoe. Some shoes may feel more comfortable on your particular feet than others, of course. But you don't really know that until you try them on, do you? So how is it that every kid and many adults I know prefer Nike brand shoes even before they try them on? Could it be the sweeping logo design? Could it be the Michael Jordan endorsement? Could it be a brand identification that is so strong that Nike forces every other sport shoe off the court? Branding impacts every product and service.

How about branding success with drinking water. I'm not talking about flavored water or soda. I mean just plain water. Without it we die and it doesn't much matter which water we drink to stay alive after a vigorous hike through the desert. But, when we dilettantes have too much time on our

Lesson 5... The Power of Branding

hands down at the local "gourmet" supermarket, we impart properties to different brands of water that they just don't have...if we are really honest about it. That is part of this branding thing.

In our own business technology sector, a study once conducted by *Reseller Management Magazine*, when I was with them, showed that 85% of our readers recommended specific product brands at the point of sale rather than generic. In my own survey of customer attitudes, we found that most buyers will ask our opinion, not indicating brand bias, but, once we make our recommendations, they then follow up with brand specific questions.

"Would there be any benefit from using an HP printer?", "Would we get better service with an Dell PC?", "Should we standardize on Microsoft Office?", "Is AT&T the right

Smart Marketing ──

choice?", etc. These are brand awareness questions that you and I face every time we make a sales presentation.

To get a better perspective on the concept of "branding", I remember a wonderful interview I once did with Ron Seredian, who was Media Relations Manager for American Power Conversion. APC is the number one brand in its market and has been for over a decade.

Prior to the interview, Ron had worked for a smaller uninterruptible power supply manufacturer that competes with APC, but one that doesn't have the brand recognition. "Wherever we went to sell battery backup, they would ask us if we sold APC when they really meant UPS. APC had so effectively branded the market that we always fought an uphill fight." Evidently, Ron didn't feel that his career path in the uninterruptible power supply business was that uninterruptible, so he moved to a winning brand name.

Apple, for a long time had practically every school teacher in America panicked that those same school teachers would be bested by their own students unless they got their schools to standardize on classroom MACs, which they felt were easier than PCs and easy enough even for Education majors to master. So, most schools bought MACs. IBM and Compaq eventually caught up, thanks to the way Microsoft Windows recaptured ease-of-use mindshare – a branding play.

You can think of hundreds of cases where branding has played a part. Those successful people at Priceline.com use branding quite successfully to capture mindshare awareness through extensive marketing of William Shattner's "I told you this will be big… really big."

Just what is a "brand image", how does it work to create a buying psychology and how can small companies use branding to improve sales numbers? I asked Andrew F. Kallfelz, who

Lesson 5... The Power of Branding

was Business Unit Manager at American Power Conversion. Kallfelz has spent much of his education and business life thinking about branding. He starts by defining a brand simply as "a collection of associations that mean something to the customer". "The key," according to Kallfelz, "is to influence what those associations will be."

How do you get customers to make the associations that are most favorable to you and result in buying what you sell? According to Kallfelz, you can use symbols, sound and color to create and manage those associations, but, to accomplish your selling objective, you need to ask yourself:

1. What do you want the associations with your brand to be?
2. What do you need to say in order to have the prospect see the association you want?

Simply put, can you come up with a slogan (like Priceline.com's use of William Shattner's "...really big" and Col. Saunders "We do chicken right"), or logo (like Microsoft Windows), or color (like IBM blue or UPS brown), that derives from your mission statement and identifies only you?

Can you project something into the market that is new, specific to solving a problem, is different in some critical way, or is so darned easy to remember that it crowds every competitor out of your prospect's thoughts like they did at 1(800) FLOWERS? These are hard questions, but the answers will propel you to success faster than faster-acting Anacin (or is it Bufferin?).

Kallfelz notes that APC has been very good at doing that. In 1985 it sold its first battery backup unit and had no brand recognition at all. They worked on it and, by 1988, they climbed to $18 million in sales. Last year, as the definitive brand name in power protection, revenues topped $1 billion.

Smart Marketing

Lest you fear to take on APC, or the Goliath in your own market niche, remember that when APC started out they were 20th out of 20 producers of power-related products. Consider, too, how, several years ago everyone lamented that the processor market was as good as dead in this country. Then a branding promotion came along that said simply "Intel Inside" and look how much farther that company's market cap has come since.

The healthy thing about branding is that it can help every David to become a Goliath (making way for newer and subsequent Davids to follow). One of the newest "Davids" is Advanced Micro Devices, AMD, which has built a new and powerful brand of, well, newer and more powerful computer chips to challenge the market leader Intel. Another is Qualcomm, which kept on plugging its brand against the established giants until, suddenly, its founders went from poor to very, very rich.

Branding is not only for manufacturers, or very large companies. According to Steve Twombley, former Publisher of *Reseller Management Magazine*, there is so much volatility, margin chopping and trench warfare in sales that branding is the key to allowing small companies to rise above the fray.

> "Brand recognition provides you with credibility," said Twombley. "It highlights longevity and reliability. It provides prospects and clients with comfort about you. Branding is an important concept where you have established recognition for your own brand."

Once established, the added-value benefits of branding are huge. Future promotions are leveraged off of the recognition of your name and then even your smaller promotions bring

Lesson 5... The Power of Branding

greater returns then they would without a known brand behind them.

Brand recognition is clearly the key to ongoing success. Unfortunately, the biggest problem most small companies face is that they know of only two ways to get brand recognition:

1. Expensive.
2. More expensive.

But, this doesn't have to be the case. Although well funded companies, like Priceline.com, have used huge sums of money as an effectively short cut to quick branding success; others have established a credible brand value and loyalty via less expensive routes. Think of Yahoo, and, my favorite longshot on the outside, Red Hat Linux. These companies didn't start out with huge brand budgets, but they did start out with a strategy that would win the hearts and minds of their market with consistent and focused promotion of their respective identities.

If you cannot afford a full court press, why not enlist the support of your vendors for co-op help. Add the name of the well established branded products you sell right onto your letterhead and business cards to associate your own brand with bigger, more proven and more comforting brands. Co-op mailings, co-op advertising and other co-op promotions associate your name with quality, stability, reliability and other forms of greatness.

Beside co-op programs, it pays to consider targeting specific local or regional markets at first and grow your name geographically as you grow qualitatively. Earthlink was a local California internet access provider who has now associated with the Sprint brand and has expanded nationally, only after building a stable regional platform and name. Earthlink also

Smart Marketing

chose a brand name that didn't require lots of explaining as to what they do, which helps.

As you can see, applying branding to your marketing plan can get you out of that one-sale-at-a-time rut and into the big time. Getting back to our riddle, what's the real difference between a Hoover and a Harley? To a brand marketer, it's that Harley, still respectful of its brand franchise, is regaining its old market share. Hoover isn't.

LESSON SIX

Hair-Raising Brands
. . . . . .

A branding strategy alone won't guarantee you'll remain the market leader, but without it you'll never get there. Ways to create your brand and then keep it strong in the hearts and minds of your customers.

Do you think I should start using Rogaine to regrow hair? According to the marketing staff of the Upjohn Company, those wonderful folks who bring us Rogaine brand Minoxodil, I fondly remember an ad that said I could send for a free information kit and a $10 incentive to see a Doctor (They capitalize the D in Doctor, knowing well, where their capital is coming from).

In a full page ad in Natural History Magazine (of all places), they encouraged you and me to "do what millions have already done. Find out about Rogaine - the only natural way to regrow your own natural hair".

On an additional two-thirds page, on the back of the

Smart Marketing ――

display ad, there were hundreds of tiny, fine-print words that talked about the neurological, dermatological, gastrointestinal, cardiovascular, genital, endocrine, psychiatric, hematological and musculoskeletal side effects, but all of this too-small-for-my-eyes stuff came under a big bold heading that said "THE ONLY PRODUCT EVER PROVEN TO REGROW HAIR".

Amidst all the detailed ad copy, I did find that Upjohn provided these curiously interesting statistics based on scientific study:

- 26% of patients reported moderate hair growth after four months with Minoxodil,
- Half the number who continued using Rogaine (I guess that means somewhat less than 13%) reported continued growth after one year, and
- 11% of patients using a placebo reported moderate hair growth.

This seemed to imply to me that, of every hundred people who try Rogaine, no more than two additional people might benefit from continued use than those who use a placebo, or who don't do anything at all. Of course, the evidence does give Rogaine at least an 8.4% advantage in head-to-head tests with the placebo.

Compared with the placebo, however, Rogaine is far more expensive, appears to be more dangerous in terms of side effects and could not be taken, until recently, without prescription and constant doctors care. All this, for incrementally better results?

With those comparatives, we wonder if there is a scientifically valid case for marketing, not just the lower-priced, non-branded Minoxodil, but the actual placebo. The placebo results may prove to be almost as good and the margins, well,

Lesson 6... Hair-Raising Brands

the margins are downright terrific. If we could only give the placebo a good brand image like Rogaine has.

After all, don't we all know of people who have made successful careers starting with second-tier products at vastly reduced prices from the front runner, then building the images of those products and finally overtaking the leaders? Of course we do. And they do it, most often, with a strong branding strategy.

We discuss this in the Lesson Five, "The Power of Branding". There, we note that branding is the single most important of all marketing principles. You may not stay in first place with it, but you will never get to first place without it.

Consider, with the thousands (yes, thousands) of small companies making and selling computers, Compaq, by building a brand, managed to overtake both IBM and Apple. Then, Dell branded itself past Compaq. MicroSoft Word, although never the top choice to professional reviewers in the word processing game, by employing a brand strategy, overtook WordPerfect. UPS has overtaken FedEx. I predict that worldcom, or Sprint, will overtake the venerable AT&T.

Successful come-from-behinds learn from the leader, probe for weaknesses and are able to exploit them. Each of these successes is built on momentum created by a branding strategy.

Even pure placebo products may gain acceptance through branding, as was the case with a once well known computer memory (ram doubling) software that proved to have absolutely no effect on performance, but sold like hot-cakes until brand momentum was halted and brand good-will destroyed under full public disclosure that the product was flaky (This once happened, in politics, when Ross Perot accused the CIA of infiltrating his daughter's wedding, but, alas, that's another story.).

Smart Marketing

Moving further along, is there a lesson here that you can use to grow your own, er, market? Of course, there is, in three easy steps:

1. **In order to build a brand, you need to develop a concept of what your brand should stand for.**

    What should your prospect think of when he/she hears your brand name? Have you thought of what prospects think of when they hear your name? "The tightest ship in the shipping business" is the UPS way to imprint that they are more cost effective than FedEx.

    UPS feels it can work on the economy image, since it feels that most of us already accept its reliability. It doesn't worry about U.S. Postal Service's Priority Mail offering which lost valuable mind share when USPS had to modify its "2 dollar, 2 lbs., 2 days, guaranteed" program.

    The Postal Service blew its brand equity the day it raised its Priority Mail rate 50% the same time it rescinded its two-day delivery promise. Instantly, emulating the public relations success of Mr. Perot, it became known for "2 lbs. 3 dollars, 4 ever."

2. **After you have determined what your brand should stand for, you need to create a logo, or image, that will communicate that message to your audience.**

    Priceline.com, Microsoft, Coca Cola, UPS, et al, have spent billions to create brand awareness and recognition, but you may be able to substitute well-crafted intellectual awareness for a big marketing budget.

    Internet World Magazine tells, in its name, what it does for you. So does JiffyLube, CompUSA and 1(800)LAWYERS. The important thing to remember is that your audience must think of you whenever it thinks about any problem that you can solve.

Lesson 6... Hair-Raising Brands

Even our own Office Technology Consulting, Inc., was suffering from an image identity problem until we focused on the fact that nobody in the business had more experience and expertise in integrating telecommunications concepts than us.

We knew we were good, but our corporate identity always needed a little bit of extra explaining. This is the sales equivalent of always starting a foot race twenty feet behind the starting line.

Thus was born the "PhoneGuru™" logo to tell, in one quick word, what we brazenly thought of ourselves. This has had a marked effect on sales. Suddenly, we had a concept of what our brand should stand for and we were able to create an instant image in the minds of our prospects.

3. In order that all this good work bears fruit, you need an ongoing program that constantly develops new ways to keep your brand image in front of your prospects and clients.

    We didn't change our name, although people have suggested it, for the same reason that Bob Dole and I still refer to the Brooklyn Dodgers. I'm an old fashioned sort of guy who doesn't warm quickly to such radical acts. Instead, we embarked on a series of moves to instill the PhoneGuru(concept in the hearts and minds of our target public.

    As you know, we created the phoneguru.com website and email address (stan@phoneguru.com, etc.). That is a primary medium, which, as Marshall McLuhan said, is now our message. We include that cyber address on everything we send out: letters, faxes, business cards, promo materials. It reinforces who we are (phone gurus) and that we are well connected to the electronic frontier.

    You've been to trade shows where people line up for hours, wasting valuable shopping time, just to get a stupid shirt

Smart Marketing

with somebody else's logo on it. Well, I don't. When I'm washing the car or walking through the mall, I don't have to wear my Sprint Data shirt or my APC shirt, because I can wear my www.phoneguru.com shirt.

Our company name (which we already agree doesn't adequately define what we do) is not on it. Instead, our shirt sports the soccer ball logo of Stamford Little League Soccer, plus our web address. We sponsor a team of eight-year olds, who all wear our web address on their shirts, too.

The goal, which has been achieved, by the way, is simply to add one more layer, reinforcing the PhoneGuru™ brand to the business community, so that whenever there is a business question about telecommunications, data integration, or cabling infrastructure, business knows to come to us for answers. Also, since we are a philanthropic family, this shirt thing seems to be a good fit, so to speak.

So, to review our three simple steps for creating your own guerrilla branding campaign:

1. Develop the concept of what you want your product or service to stand for in the minds of your audience.
2. Create a logo, or image, to communicate your message to your audience.
3. Keep developing new ways to put your brand image in front of new prospects.

In addition, as we have discussed in the ram doubling case, it is important to be able to deliver quality goods to those who buy. If you cannot, your best creative efforts will not have the staying power to make the exercise worth your while. Branding will get you noticed and get your foot in the door, not insignificant achievements, by any standard, but results, in most cases, are usually required for continued brand success.

Lesson 6... Hair-Raising Brands

Unless, of course, you are selling hair-growing preparations, diet pills, or other forms of hopeware. In that case, the paradigm shifts and we can use scientific statistics to justify a run with the Minoxodil placebo.

In fact, I think I have the brand concept that capitalizes, both, on the Rogaine brand and the continuing hunger for dieting aids. Let's offer hair growth and weight loss in the same bottle, two for the price of one. We'll call it "NOGAIN!" and, since it is a total placebo with a guarantee of no side effects, our universally acceptable message can be: "No pain! NOGAIN!"

LESSON SEVEN

Jordan, Tiger, Hot Dogs & You
- - - - - -

There's a lot more to pricing than figuring percentages over cost. The key marketing concepts that will shape your marketing strategies and multiply your margins.

Y ou can learn a lot about marketing from a summertime hot dog. I learned this some fifteen, or so, years ago, but the lesson still holds true. Back then, I was entrusted with putting together a picnic style party for a bunch of swells from our local yacht club.

We were to sail out to some remote spot, drop anchor, lash the boats together in one wide raft, and party. What must I do, I thought? What must I buy? What should I feed them? I obsessed a lot, back then.

"Make it simple," somebody told me, "All we need is a bunch of nice napkins, some hot dogs and a lot of beer. It can be catered for under fifteen bucks a head."

SMART MARKETING ——

Sounds like a plan, I thought. But I did not end up calling a caterer for that party. I mean, how can you, in good conscience, call a caterer to order hot dogs for gosh sakes? Instead, I dropped in on the regional Sabrette hot dog wholesaler who showed me how to do it for less than two bucks per...so inexpensive, I am almost too ashamed to confess it.

Ordinarily, this discount buying never would have occurred to me, except that the Sabrette folks were right next door to my accountant's office building and, well, I thought, let's just see what "wholesale" really means.

Buying without the retail markup really clarified, for me, the marketing concept of pricing strategy. Here was the cost breakdown per person:

- 2 All beef hot dogs = .20
- 2 Rolls = .20
- Sauerkraut = .02
- Mustard = .00000002
- Baked beans = .06
- Chips = .14
- Beer/soda (average) = .48
- Fancy paperware = .06
- Total cost per person = $1.16000002.

The costs were so low that I replaced the beer with champagne and we really had a grand time afloat.

When laid out this way, aren't you amazed at the retail economics of food? I am. I can recall that a quick hot dog on a roll, which costs about 21 cents WITHOUT the beer, has cost me anywhere from a buck and a quarter at the lunch truck down the street, to $2.80 at O'Hare International Airport...which I was more than willing to pay before learning

Lesson 7... Jordan, Tiger, Hot Dogs & You

that the hot dog markup at O'Hare is big enough to earn the restaurant owner his own short order airport.

These margins kinda make you think that it's really not too late to buy stock in companies like McDonalds, doesn't it? The lesson of the hot dog is that some products, in some markets, evidently, are a lot easier to sell at much higher gross margins than others:
1. If your customers are hungry enough for what you've got,
2. If they perceive strong relative value, and
3. If you have positioned yourself as being the one who delivers the goods.

Of course, there's always a component of overhead between cost of goods and final sale price; but, the difference between a bad business and a good one may just be your failure to recognize that by charging just a bit more, you can use the increased profit to improve your brand marketing effort, so you then can charge a little more, and then improve marketing more, and so on, and so on.

Look, for instance, at how Nike has built its marketing budget by expanding the spread between low cost of product and high retail price until it seems not to matter how much they charge anymore.

How much will Michael Jordan and Tiger Woods receive together from Nike? About a hundred million dollars a year? Add to that, the agency and media cost of advertising and promotion in order to carry these spokespersons' messages to the public. Maybe that's another two hundred mil, or so, all paid from its expanded spread between cost and retail.

Nike sells about $3 billion each year, or about 30 million pairs of hundred dollar sneakers (more or less). If my very rough and totally unscientific math is anywhere close to the

53

Smart Marketing

money, here is how I figure the cost of sales broken down per pair of shoes*:

- Jordan, Woods, et al   = 10
- Shoe store and salesman   = 45
- General and Administrative and profits   = 34
- Materials   = 07
- Manufacturing and shipping   = 01
- Third world shoemaker labor   = 03
- **Total retail price**   = $100+

Notice that, in our simple-minded analysis of the relative values of this hypothetical, maybe eleven percent goes into the cost of building the product and five and a half times that goes into brand building and sales.

(*NOTE: This is only my hypothetical, non-scientific, tongue in cheek, pedagogical analysis. Nike is really a nice company. Also, do not use these figures as a basis for your own business plan — Duhh.)

Let's not single out Nike, or Sabrette. What do you think it costs to produce a box full of WIN95 or NT? How much is a half-ounce of colored powder like the kind that Estee Lauder (or equivalent) might sell for $184 at Macy's?

What the lesson of the hot dog teaches is that you can sell something at a great multiple of its original. Like everything else we discuss here, this is not new, is not unique and is not beyond your reach if you understand these three marketing concepts that help build great margins:

Lesson 7... Jordan, Tiger, Hot Dogs & You

CONCEPT ONE
Price services based on customer value, rather than on cost basis.

This means that you should strive to determine the value to your customer rather than simply marking up your cost of the product. If the value is great...great. Mark it up. If the value is not, maybe you're in the wrong business.

The other day, I wanted to buy a book as a gift for a friend's new baby. The book I wanted lists for $17.95. By surfing the net I found that both Amazon.com and BN.com (formerly barnesandnoble.com) sell that same book, but, because they are deeply involved in a cutthroat price war, guess what? They retail it for the same $17.95.

What? No break from these big drum-banging discounters? Of course not. These savvy webmasters already know that, although they may hype their discount pitch 'til my screen freezes over, neither one of them has any interest in discounting all of the million or so books that are cataloged for sale.

The more value to me, the more they charge. That's the secret behind hotel room pricing, airline tickets and dinner on

SMART MARKETING

New Year's Eve. Is everyone else but you pricing this way? Time to get with the program.

CONCEPT TWO
Do some active brand building.

This is the process we've talked about in Lesson Five, when Andrew F. Kallfelz, Business Unit Manager at American Power Conversion defined a brand simply as "a collection of associations that mean something to the customer. "The key", according to Kallfelz, was "to influence what those associations will be."

To me, the brands associated with "new book" are Amazon.com and BN.com, so that's where I looked to buy one. To a kid looking for a pair of cool shoes, the association has become Nike due to the celebrity representation by Michael and Tiger. To a woman who wants to cover her face with colored chalk, or a man who wants to splash on some smelly water, it may be one of the Estee Lauder brands.

But branding and brand management are not only for the big guys with big marketing budgets. Your own prospects and customers may be subtly influenced to associate you with their need for your product or service, which will lead them to call you first.

You become branded at the local level by sponsoring little league teams and local business breakfasts, by repeatedly mailing, phoning and advertising to the same people, and by becoming known in the market we operate as being steady, reliable and valuable. Remember, your goal is to influence the mental associations of prospects and existing customers.

CONCEPT THREE
Set deliverable standards of excellence in your market.

This is the final leg of this tripod. We can easily see why Sun and Microsoft battle over web standards. Each company's

Lesson 7... Jordan, Tiger, Hot Dogs & You

"standards" may not meet the global community's goals for standardization. But "standards", in marketing circles, can often mean delivering non-standardized features and benefits competitors can only dream of.

3Com has leveraged its lead by driving forward with its proprietary Palm Pilot non-standardized standard that is different from the rest of the pack. If it can show better functional value, it will keep its margins up...way up.

American Power Conversion does that with a sleek set of software tools that communicate between the APC uninterruptible power supplies and the electronics they protect. I can never remember the names of these products, but I do know that they monitor power and warn network users well before failure and they automatically power down systems in a controlled, organized fashion...but only on APC systems, maintaining brand value for APC.

At the local level, these are marketing concepts you can use. I once met a lawyer in White Plains, NY, who applied all three of these concepts in his very lucrative one-man practice. He set the local standard of excellence in his "market" by becoming known in the legal community as the most knowledgeable and successful attorney at winning traffic arguments. He branded himself well, since just about everyone in town thought of him whenever they thought of a traffic violation.

It's not arguing before the Supreme Court, to be sure, but it made this guy one heck of a niche-market living. He

Smart Marketing

extended his "Brand" by reinforcing himself in the eyes of other attorneys as the only resource an attorney should refer to a client who got a really nasty traffic ticket.

Finally, he never charged by the hour, which is the "cost-based" formula most of us are accustomed to charging. Instead, he "value priced" his service based on the offense.

"Did your lawyer tell you how I work?" he inquired the first and only time I called him. "Send me the summons and meet me in court at the appointed date and time. For your offense, my fee will cost you $400. Bring a check."

I met him in court. I paid him. We won. Subsequently, I thanked my regular attorney for the fine referral and successful conclusion. I don't remember this traffic attorney's name, or what he looks like, but he doesn't need me to so long as my attorney does.

To my mind, this attorney is narrowly focused and a positive marketing genius.

LESSON EIGHT

Advertising Specialties that Work
. . . . . .

There's a right way, and a wrong way, to distribute trinkets. How to turn specialty gifts from cheap trinkets to grand image builders.

Advertising Specialties? Trinkets for the taking? Who dug up such a notion? Our office coffee cupboard is filled with enough logo-laden mugs to host a caffeine addicts' convention, but don't ask me to recall the names.

I keep harping in these pages on the value of marketing research, but if you won't do that, before you spend another buck on another paper clip dispenser, would you at least ask the other folks around the office if they've ever saved the dozens of paper clip dispensers THEY get every year? Then ask the one guy who actually kept his if he ever bought anything from the guy that gave it to him.

Once, at a spring computer reseller show, I was privileged to attend yet another seminar opportunity and I got to wend my way up and down the exhibition aisles, scooping up literature; but also pens, pencils, buttons and bows from dozens

SMART MARKETING

of companies who are not yet household words and perhaps never will be.

Incredibly, many exhibitors at these events mark their goodies with neither descriptions of what they do, nor phone numbers, nor even towns of origin, should I become ever so curious as to seek them out on general principle (and, alas, what other reason could I possibly have for running down these faceless names?). Certainly, free samples of what they do would make more sense, wouldn't it?

At one PC EXPO where I was speaking, one company gave out real cute key rings. Tiny battery operated attachments made sounds of sirens, machine guns and aerial bombardments that recreated World War II, which is fine for those who need more excitement in their pockets. But neither the key ring nor its container identified the donor, so I gave it away to my favorite four year-old without guilt. I once received a package in the mail, a tape of Reba McEntire's latest songs. I love it, but, for the life of me, I can't tell you who sent it. I don't know what quid is expected for this quo.

I'm impressed. I'm thankful. But who sent this...and why? There's more. Several years ago, I received a laser disk of modern jazz that I gave away, never having heard it, because, at that time, I hadn't advanced with civilization's march on digital sound and didn't have a laser disk player.

How embarrassing. Not only have I been paid off without an inkling as to why, but also I've been paid off in merchandise that is as useful to me as frequent flier miles to serial killer, lifetime convict, Charlie Manson. I have since purchased a laser player, have received other disks and now know that my benefactor of that first disk is the incredibly talented jazz artist, former CEO of Borland, Phillippe Kahn...His career is in the tank and now he tells me!

In our effort to be sophisticated in our handling of gifts,

Lesson 8... Advertising Specialties that Work

we sometimes tend to do things that are maybe a wee bit too subtle for our own good.

If you want to give away things, you need to think through a marketing strategy as though you were selling the items for real money. Otherwise, people will throw them away and nobody wins.

The best advertising-specialty campaign I ever saw was so good that the week I received my gift I plagiarized the concept and ran a program just like it. Here's how it worked.

First, I received a mailing telling me that the president of this company was very impressed with a handy, new letter opener. He said that he found it very useful and that he wanted me to have one like his, and promised to send it within a week, or so.

The following week, I received a second mailing, extolling the virtues of this exciting letter opener and included, not just one, but two, of them. "I know that your secretary will have her eye on yours," he said, "and it's ludicrous for you to have it, while she continues to open your mail the hard way. So here's one for her, too."

He didn't give me a letter opener. He didn't give me two. He SOLD them to me, just as if he would if he had planned to bill me for them. He took a $1.00 item and built a campaign around it that embossed his name in my memory forever.

How many times have you wondered if you were wasting good money by sending things to people? Well, here's the scoop: If you didn't sell it, or make a big deal out of it, you probably did waste your money.

I have, on occasion, said that I didn't think that advertising specialties were always a big waste, but I have implied that they often are. There's a place for specialty advertising in the marketing world, but not as cheap throwaways which only serve to reinforce the image of low-margin, commodity supplies.

Smart Marketing ——

Finding a useful gift, however, bringing it to the attention of your customers and prospects, and explaining its functionality and usefulness...well that's the image that is well worth cultivating.

LESSON NINE

Newsletters can Restart Marketing Engines
. . . . . .

This low-cost, easy-to-implement program provides better than average ROI. A ten-point plan for newsletter marketing success.

Use newsletters to restart your marketing engine. We do this with a fall newsletter which is low in cost, easy to implement and provides a much better than average ROI.

If you haven't kept in touch over the summer, fall is a great time to contact every friend, client and associate in your corporate database, personal correspondence file and Palm Pilot® phone list.

A corporate newsletter is professionally prepared and sent to everybody in your database. Its goals are to remind everyone that:

1. You are still in business and are looking for new clients,
2. That you still improve office productivity and lower operating costs,

Smart Marketing ──

3. That you have a great guarantee, and
4. That you have a fall special to announce.

To ensure that your newsletter is successful and reaches your intended audience, we adhere to the following 10 points and suggest that you do, too:

1. Prepare an interesting lead article that is meant to teach and/or assist your reader in an obviously profitable way.

This is the reader "bribe" to ensure that the newsletter isn't tossed into the recycle bin (at least immediately). If you can't write really useful and interesting stuff, be honest with yourself and hire a writer.

Hiring a writer is not such a new concept. You hire phone canvassers and sales people to create the oral words that will sell for you. So why not hire good people to create written words, as well? A well-received lead article is often the difference between a newsletter's success and failure.

2. Keep the prose short, but conversational.

Think of newsletter articles as "sound bites" for the eye. Include lots of good ideas that are representative of what you can do.

Examples from our own files include:

- How we saved Sam Smith $10,000 per month and cut his phone bill in half,
- We turned an ordinary PC into an 8-trunk voice-mail system for Jones & Co.,
- Upgrading your data network? Consider this first,
- NT versus Linux: where we stand, and
- Checklist for installing a new database.

Remember that this is the MTV generation, so you need to compress your ideas and get 'em out quickly, or they won't be read.

Lesson 9... Newsletters can Restart Marketing Engines

3. **Start with good artistic design.**

Most people decide to read a newsletter based on what it looks like, not what is in it. Let's face it. Until you read the article, you haven't a clue if it's any good. The articles need to be high quality, but only *after* the reader has decided to read them.

Keep the page layout simple and up to date. Those tombstone looking templates of most low-end desk-top-publishing packages just scream out to your reader "I'm boring! Throw me away." Designing a format that can be repeated often is only a one-shot deal, so hiring an artist can be really cost effective.

Speaking of design, do you know what makes a newsletter really stand out as an amateur home-made job that's hard to read? It's 10-point type, two or three column, left and right justified, and no white space. Some folks increase the type size to 12 point to make reading easier, but, guess what? That only makes things worse, because you end up typing right to the line borders to fit everything in.

If you are setting your own type, try moving down to 9.5 points, or 9 points and/or going to four columns with extra white space around lines. Don't justify the right margin, and leave a few blank spots on the page to give the reader's eye a break.

We have found that smaller type is often easier to read. Another benefit of smaller type is that, because we now can get all we want to say onto one 8 1/2 X 11 – double-sided sheet, the newsletter appears to be less demanding of our readers' time. The response is good and it's more cost effective, too.

4. Please, please, PULLEESE don't print your newsletter on your office copier or laser printer...unless, of course, you are sending it out to a prospect list of second-grade school teachers.

Smart Marketing

Your audience hasn't seen or heard from you in months and this graphic is in lieu of a premise visit. If you wouldn't think of showing up in person without a suit, or socks, don't send out a poorly dressed newsletter. The results are the same.

5. Speaking of being well dressed, print on coated (glossy), or other high quality paper that will "clothe" your newsletter in a garment that engenders respect.

6. Include your name and address both on the front and the back, so that, if your reader decides to photocopy an article for a friend, your name gets carried along like seeds on the fall wind.

If you think that this is obvious, pick through today's incoming mail and note how many times this rule is missed.

7. Include a brief summary on page one of what's inside and why it is important to the reader.

8. Include really professional photographs of yourself and/or your staff.

Here is something I never knew worked so well until I became associated with Reseller Management Magazine. I'd been writing, literally, for decades, with some degree of success. But, after this magazine hired a really great professional photographer to take a picture for my column, my reader response took a dramatic leap that defies belief.

Since then, I include my picture with everything I send out, and, you know what? It works! Take a look at this book cover and see for yourself. Don't you feel more at ease reading this, knowing what I look like?

Old friends call in responses to my photos to chide me about my aging bald head. Total strangers are more willing to

Lesson 9... Newsletters can Restart Marketing Engines

take my calls because they can pick up my newsletter and look straight into my eyes. It's a comforting feeling to potential clients to know what their caller (me) looks like.

9.   **Include something that requires an active reader response.**

It can be a questionnaire. It can be a mail-in coupon for more information about something. It can be a contest. Reader response forces the reader to switch gears at some point. It creates a jolt to the attention center.

10.   **Don't forget your advertisement.**

After all, you are paying for all this advice, aren't you? Your reader knows that if you were taking him to lunch, it wouldn't be free either, so summarize what it is that you do for money, include one or more special deals and create a call for action.

Once your newsletter is finished and mailed, is it Miller time? Noooo. The newsletter is only stage one. Our next step is to prepare a second mailing to everyone in our database with whom we are on a close first-name basis. I do this not for the marketing value, but because I am interested in these people and want to keep up the personal dialog. Nevertheless, the marketing value is there, sort of as a bonus.

For this very exclusive group, which in my case comes to about a hundred names, I used to send out a few snapshots of interesting vacation places I had been to. Now, with the advent of the cheap scanner and the internet, I arrange a few interesting color snaps on a website and, I print them out for mailing to those who are important to me. Voila! Instant Scrapbook.

I include a note with each copy asking my reader to do the same in return mail, so I can be brought up to date on his

SMART MARKETING

or her summer, too. The personal correspondence is more targeted and more personal than the corporate newsletter, and usually results in a phone call, either incoming or outgoing, to sort of reconnect with everyone after the summer.

It's a lot like the way we used to meet up with everyone back at school in the fall. Relationships are rekindled and business returns to usual. It's all kind of charming, don't you think?

LESSON TEN

Your Stationery Should Sell, Too

• • • • • •

Your wastebasket is filled with bad business stationery. Learn from this. Eight tips for making a better printed impression.

*T*ake this test. Look in your wastebasket and select five previously discarded letterheads and envelopes from the days' junk mail. Choose them at random, but look them over carefully. Chances are that your response to them will be as follows:

- You really like the design of only one of them.
- You could live with the designs of two of them.
- You feel that the senders of the remaining two probably would have been more successful at improving their images simply by replacing what they sent you with copies of their current parole records.

Smart Marketing

You think your materials are much better? So you say. Most everyone I know thinks his or her own business stationery conveys just the right marketing image. That's why they chose it. They paid for it. They use it. Yet, these folks usually are less than thrilled with the look and image conveyed by almost everybody else's material. I'm no different.

I did a little of this marketing research through my own round file recently. Of course I was careful to close my office door so I wouldn't be seen doing it (employees can be so cruel when they catch you in the trash). After checking two or three wastebaskets, I was amazed at how awful all of this obviously expensive printed stuff seemed to me.

You feel that way too? So tell me, how come you and I are such graphics geniuses while everybody else seems to have the style and flair of Homer Simpson? Could it be that Homer isn't so dumb? Maybe we're not so great at this, after all. Maybe some of the material we send out isn't getting a response that's any better than the stuff you and I routinely discard.

The lesson here is that it doesn't matter what YOU think of your stationery. What matters is that the people you mail to are impressed by it...and moved to action by it. If you want to improve your image, don't ask yourself. Don't ask an artist. Ask your customers and prospects. Let's face it, who else matters besides the guy who writes the checks?

If you ask them, customers and prospects will tell you how your material measures up to the image standard you have set. Moreover, they will tell you something even more important: Would they read your stuff if it came in the mail? Let's face it, readability interest is the key to all marketing tests.

But back to our own test of the wastebasket discards. Let's continue. Take the one letterhead in five that you liked from the test at the top of this column and try running it through the copier. How do you like it this time? Not so hot any more?

Lesson 10... Your Stationary Should Sell, Too

Well, if you really want to hate it, try looking at it from the receiving end of a FAX machine. UGGGH. If that letterhead wasn't specifically designed to withstand the rigors of today's electronic office, then it's probably pretty ugly by this point.

Keep in mind that more and more of your materials are being processed through hot, hot laser printers, then cycled through FAX machines and, finally, recycled a third time through copiers. This not only flattens fancy printing, but gives color a real black eye.

Paper, too, is an important consideration in image making, but not in the way you think. A while back, one of the more aggressive "alternative toner" companies sent me a series of computer-generated, laser-printed letters, highlighting their "highest quality toner at lowest prices".

Unfortunately, they weren't on their own mailing list and never saw the damage that their high image, high price paper was causing them. Because the very expensive paper was highly textured, it didn't hold the toner very well and by the time the letters got through the Disneyland experience we call the Postal Service, many of the characters actually had been shaken off the pages like this:

SU MER SPECI L ON ONER CARTR GES!
TOP QUALIT AT LOW, LO PRICES.

Boy, what a great selling tool for toner. After reading this, wouldn't you want to run right out and stock up on brand X toner? Me neither.

Lesson: The next time you do an important mailing, put your own name to your favorite merge file, send yourself a set of whatever your customers and prospects are getting, and you'll really learn about your image.

Smart Marketing

This doesn't mean that you shouldn't do quality printing on quality paper, but it does mean that you must consider all the alternatives for times that you will need a good paper image and for times that you won't. Remember:

- Your graphics should FAX and copy well.
- Your material shouldn't leave raised letter residue to gum up your laser printer or copy machines.
- Your paper should be able to hold on to laser print toner through the mail.

These are just a few basics that, if not addressed, will mess up even the best of designs.

According to my most powerful mentor, the U.S. Army, a map is defined as "a graphical representation of a portion of the earth's surface, drawn to scale, as seen from above." I remember repeating this to my training sergeant in a mantra-like drone and I never forgot it.

Your letterhead, business card, FAX cover sheet, etc., are graphical representations of a portion of your own piece of earth, not drawn to scale, perhaps, but definitely seen from those sufficiently "above" to be in a position to pay you real money for your time and efforts... that is, if they are suitably impressed by your graphical representation of your firm. Face it, the graphic representation

Lesson 10... Your Stationary Should Sell, Too

you send them is the only tangible image of your business that some of them will ever know.

Speaking of FAX cover sheets, by the way, if you really want to get noticed, don't use them. Face it, from a marketing standpoint, cover sheets come in two basic varieties:

1. Boringly ordinary and
2. Cutesy unprofessional.

From a "green" standpoint they are environmentally wasteful. From an accounting standpoint, they are costly three ways:

1. They use up paper,
2. They use up telephone time, and
3. They take up clerical time.

From a management standpoint, it makes no sense to send:

> THIS PAGE IS TO TELL YOU THAT
> ANOTHER PAGE FOLLOWS.

Who thought up cover sheets, anyway? Paper companies? AT&T?

Want to make a good marketing impression via FAX? Just prepare a regular letter, on a regular letterhead and, in the upper right, instead of the usual date, type the capital letters: SENT BY FAX ON XX/XX/XX. Somewhere (in the letterhead, I hope), include a return FAX number. No cover sheet. No envelope. No stamp. No waste. Good citizenship. Good economics.

So, to summarize, here are a few items for developing a good stationery image:

Smart Marketing

DO:
1. Write down what you think your image should be,
2. Ask your customers if they agree,
3. Ask anyone who receives mail or FAX from you if your stationery reflects your image,
4. Ask anyone who receives FAX material from you, to photocopy it and send back the photocopies for your quality review, and
5. Mail to yourself so you can see the damage you are doing to yourself, first hand.

DON'T:
1. Print stationery that will not copy well,
2. Print with raised lettering, or use paper that suffers laser printing poorly, or
3. Use wasteful FAX cover sheets.

Stationery is your office to those who never come to visit you. Letterheads are like unfurnished rooms in your office that take on whole new appearances when they have been furnished with words, charts and tables instead of desks and credenzas. It is only after you have seen these "rooms" filled with "furniture" that you can get that warm, strong, comfortable feeling you seek to convey.

LESSON ELEVEN

The Real Value of Market Research
. . . . . .

Look closely at your market, and rewards will follow. Four keys from a Yale Ph.D. on how to get the answers you need.

 Seek and ye shall find. If you take the time to look closely at your market, you will be rewarded with business. Market research is a lot like periodically taking your blood pressure. A slight elevation in blood pressure, while nothing to get overly concerned about, gives you a timely hint that unhealthy life-style changes may be starting to occur and you should consider small steps now that will avoid the need for more intensive treatment later.

 Similarly, periodically sampling your target population will alert you when your prospects and clients begin changing their wants and needs while there is still time for you to adapt to those changes. Market research, like taking blood pressure, is

Smart Marketing

easy to do, but requires knowledge for thorough understanding and interpretation. As with taking your own blood pressure, you can benefit by performing self-exams between doctor visits.

According to Dr. Ronnie Braun, a market research specialist who holds a Ph.D. from Yale, "market research", with proper professional guidance, is a very accurate way to learn what people really feel about issues. Dr. Braun suggests four important aspects to keep in mind:

1. **Sample the right population.**

If you want to find out what people think about electronic mail applications, you have to ask people who, at least, know what that means. You can try sampling part of your existing customer base, for instance, to find the characteristics that are common to them. This can help you identify others who fit the same profile. Instead of random prospecting, you can begin to target your market for more improved sales results.

2. **Use appropriate statistical methods to analyze the data.**

Question only 10 people and you may get a trend about what is happening. You will not get definitive percentages, because you have too small a sample to be statistically accurate, but the trend will point you in the right selling direction. Many of us have been taught to ask prospects who didn't buy "why not?", but we rarely do the kind of research that tells us which prospects we should avoid in the first place. Statistical analysis of failed attempts could reduce wasted selling time and improve sales productivity.

3. **Ask the right questions.**

If you want to find out if members of the local Chamber of Commerce are suitable prospects, don't ask questions that waste time (questions that you already know the answers to), questions that the prospects or customers find boring, personal

Lesson 11... The Real Value of Market Research

questions, or questions that are too general. Here are good market research questions: What would you like to see? What could we invent for you? What are your biggest problems and how are your needs being met or not being met by the marketplace? What works well for you? What frustrates you? What changes in our business do you like most, least?

Choosing the right list of clients or prospects will be of limited use if you fail to get the right people within the target firms. Okay, so have you really taken a close look to see if what you sell is really desired by most of the people you sell to? If not, form several focus groups. In market research circles, focus groups are hot. The concept is faster, lower in cost and easier to accomplish than large statistical studies. You won't get detailed study percentages, but a focus group definitely will tell you the needs of your customers and how to service them better. Here's how to run a focus group:

1. Assemble lists of the groups you think have sales potential. These can be existing customers, prospects, failed sales presentations, new and untested verticals, etc.
2. Choose a small sampling from each group for a "focus group" session. Determine what you want to accomplish and learn from this group before the meeting. Why did they buy, or not buy? What would they want to buy from you if you could sell it to them?

Smart Marketing

3. Ask them interesting starter questions and give them freedom to really "open up." Don't ask new questions before finishing up with old ones and let everyone have his say. Don't provide answers or rebuttals. You're here to learn.
4. Cover all of your agenda areas of concern before ending the session.
5. Tabulate, organize and evaluate your answers.

Sometimes market research means nothing more than sifting through and making sense of the data that is right in front of you. My friends John and Kay have data, but not answers. John is a New York City VAR who sells PC-based voicemail and interactive voice response systems. He says he provides great service and customers love him. "Our service renewal rate is very high," he enthuses. One of John's customers recently asked me to recommend a replacement service vendor, because John's service was "not so hot" and that his price was too high. When I told John, his response was that service was great, but the customer failed to provide a dedicated test line. "I asked for that line months ago," John protested. Has John lost touch with his accounts?

Like John, Kay has been selling her own proprietary (now PC-based) telephone call accounting systems to telephone installation companies for over a decade. She won't sell to Howie, because he hasn't paid his bill. Howie stopped buying from Kay, because he lost two good accounts over lousy installations with her equipment, which is now sitting in a corner of his warehouse gathering dust, waiting for an return merchandise authorization and pickup, which may never come. John and Kay run high seven-figure businesses, but each is continuing down a path of illusionary management.

Dr. Braun knows that facing the emotional truth in business, as in our personal lives, is not without pain and, that, not

Lesson 11... The Real Value of Market Research

everyone has the honesty and emotional stability to conduct his or her own market research project in which case nothing less than professional help will do.

If you can face the hard truth, then you can run your own simple projects and get a lot out of them; or you can hire a market research team; or you can collaborate. However, if you are like John or Kay, you may be too close to the forest to see those damaged trees. If so, be honest; the marketing doctor advises: take two aspirin and call her in the morning.

LESSON TWELVE

Garbage In–Garbage Out.
. . . . . .

If you want meaningful data, ask the right questions. Potato growers get it right. Our Department of Commerce doesn't.

Market research reports can turn up the most fascinating insights about your relationships with your customers and their actual mindset regarding the image that you are trying so hard to create. I turn your attention to one such study revealed on National Public Radio, recently, that had been conducted by The Idaho Potato Council.

This trade association, it seems, conducted a well-devised and well-funded survey (as we have been preaching for you to perform every now and then) in an attempt to better define its brand image.

They asked a representative group of potato eaters if they knew where Idaho potatoes came from. Only 58%, if you can

SMART MARKETING ──

believe it, opined that the well-known spuds came from Idaho. We didn't hear where the other 42% thought the Idaho potato came from, but it does give one pause for thought.

Jay Leno, that great market researcher (in my opinion), teaches a wonderful nightly marketing seminar he calls "Jay walking" (if you are open to being educated after the late night news). The night before the Idaho radio report, Leno took to the streets to interview several young Americans, as part of his show and as one of his regular segments.

On this particular night, it was the African-American's turn, and Leno's question was, "What do the letters NAACP stand for?" Twelve out of twelve of Leno's interviewees had no clue.

It must be pointed out that Leno was not taking aim specifically at African-Americans. It was just their turn in the Leno batting order that has featured in past segments just about every age, sex, education and ethnic group with similar questions that we think each respective group can answer and similar results wherein they cannot.

Leno then asked several white youths the date that slavery was abolished in America. One guy answered 1941. Another volunteered that it was 1981. Nobody got the answer right, or even was within the correct century. This is not only very funny, but it is very instructional about misplaced assumptions.

The next time you start making assumptions about what members of your own market niche think, I say hold on a minute. Think about the 42% who don't know where Idaho potatoes come from, or remind yourself of the many common interest groups that don't respond as expected to Leno's questions. Maybe you should survey your market more often and learn what your customers and prospects are really thinking. This could greatly improve your marketing results.

Lesson 12... Garbage In-Garbage Out.

Our very own United States Department of Commerce is big on surveys. They are performed by the Bureau of the Census. I don't think that they are as good at finding out stuff as the Idaho potato people are, however. You be the judge.

A few months ago I received a letter from "the Bureau" that said: "The Economic Census, taken every 5 years provides our **single most important measure of our nation's economic performance.** These data are essential to business and government decision making. We need information about your company to provide reliable data for your industry and geographic area." The letter went on to advise me that Title 13 United States Code requires response to this census.

Since you and I are paying these Census Bureau folks, I thought you might like to benefit from the fruits of this high-value research service, so here is a reprint of the entire census survey I received recently from that well-trained Bureau of the Census.

1a. Is this establishment's physical location the same as the address shown in the label?
1b. Is this establishment physically located inside the legal boundaries of the city, town, village, etc.?
1c. In what type of municipality is this establishment physically located?
1d. In what county...?
2. (Check off) Kind of Business or activity.
3. CERTIFICATION - This report is substantially accurate and has been prepared in accordance with instructions.

There was a place for me to date and sign the census form and a reply envelope to mail it back in.

Imagine! Our government needs me to verify that my address is within a certain town and county. This, and our SIC

SMART MARKETING

code, is all they need to complete the search for the "**single most important measure of our nation's economic performance**".

Now I don't like to complain, but I don't think that this is the kind of information-gathering survey that tells us very much. I believe that Jay Leno's questions tell us much more that can be useful about our market than the Census Bureau's questions do.

The census, in fact, asked questions that can be answered from the Federal Tax Return and a good city-county database program. I think that if I were conducting a census, after all the printing and mailing, I might add a question or two about number of employees (and if there was any growth projected), or what amount of business was being done overseas. Maybe you can think of a question or two, yourself.

Before we jump to conclusions about only government people missing good market research opportunities, thumb through today's batch of incoming unsolicited mail that you were about to toss in the round file. Here, you can pick out lots of real cases that will be as instructive to you as a graduate MBA course.

For me, comparing and contrasting these different types of communications is not only helpful, it's fun. So, here's another marketing case history for you to ponder.

Reuters America, Inc., as we all read, had been facing some marketing setbacks stemming, in part, from a criminal indictment alleging, I believe, that it had hired a computer VAR to hack the computers and spy on its competitor, Bloomberg News Service. For balance, no doubt, Reuters was determined to assist its customers by creating a "year 2000" solution - a great marketing move for anyone.

The Reuters letter to customers was really much, much longer than the U.S. Business Census, so I won't bore you with

Lesson 12... Garbage In-Garbage Out.

all of it. However, this extract, while edited for space, is not, in my opinion, out of context. It will give you some marketing food for thought:

"Dear _____,

"The year 2000 not only marks the beginning of a new Millennium but also represents a formidable challenge for computer systems everywhere. For Reuters, the challenge is both complex and detailed, and involves coordinating with our several thousand data sources and suppliers of hardware, software and other services...

"Our Millennium Compliance Programme was established to address millennium issues in our products...Although the Millennium itself is still more than two years away, we believe it is important to tell you now about our programme, so that we can begin to work constructively with you to address issues relating to your Reuters installation...

"As a result, we have decided to make obsolete a number of products ahead of the Millennium and to withdraw support for them no later than 31 December 1999."

In other words, they solved the double zero problem by zeroing out their service.

The letter went on to note all of the products that would need to be replaced by new ones and listed almost 100 products and services, on three pages of single spaced entries, that they will have deemed obsolete within six months of the letter, as of December 31, 1999. Some solution.

Now that's what I call an interesting marketing letter. Reuters is a pretty big marketing operation, of course, but it

SMART MARKETING ──

does cross my mind that a little well-placed market research here could have gone a long way in helping them present a more pleasing, shall we say, user interface.

What could they do differently? Well, for starters, they could do with a bit of attitude adjustment and start viewing their customers as partners, just as I think we all should.

After all, if you have a strategic partnering arrangement with another company, or companies, you don't usually make fundamental changes without conferring with your partners first. Why not treat your customers and prospects the same way?

After the Reuters letter had stated the obvious regarding the year 2000 problem, it could have presented their doomsday solution as only a preliminary possibility and asked for proactive subscriber comments. This would have:

1. Empowered customers with a chance to ventilate their concerns.
2. Given the vendor a better understanding of what the market feels and needs.
3. Possibly created a few harvestable solutions.
4. Minimized damage from adverse public relations.

So, as you can see, market research, if done right, not only can provide vital intelligence that will show what your customers really think, want, and will buy...all the basics of good brand building, it can also be used to reach out to your customer base to build rapport, bringing them closer to you and farther away from the competition.

Just about a decade ago, everybody and his brother flooded the mail with company newsletters of varying artistic and aesthetic quality, handily crafted with new (at the time) laser printers and Windows GUI software. We're more grown up, now, and have interactive tools like the internet, fax-back,

Lesson 12... Garbage In-Garbage Out.

etc., making it easier than ever to turn one-way communications into two-way dialog with our prospects and customers.

It is easier than ever to listen to your market and learn fascinating new things. Do it.

It works in Idaho.

LESSON THIRTEEN

Talk is Cheap
· · · · · ·

> Horror stories about stuff that doesn't work, and how the market reacts. Does your product measure up to what you promise? Does it really matter?

I once had a client, we'll call him Joe, who's in the focus group business. His staff gathers groups of folks like you and me into one of his many conference rooms and asks us a lot of questions about products such as, "Do you like this smooth peanut butter, or do you prefer the chunky?"

Each conference room is separated from a poshly-appointed, raised-floor viewing room by a one-way glass mirror where clients, and others who enjoy watching people at work, can see and listen to people who have peanut butter stuck to

Smart Marketing ——

the tops of their mouths, for instance. Because the subjects cannot see you, you can also feel free to identify the perpetrator without fear of reprisals.

Joe once sent me a fax that said, in part, that everything we do from here on out MUST be "year 2000 compliant". He sent the same fax to the guy running the telephone cables in his walls. He sent one to the electrician. He sent one to the building owner who was installing the sheet-rock walls for new offices. He sent the year 2000 compliance notice to everyone, including, and I only have this on hearsay, the deli man at the lunch counter down the street.

You might think that Joe was a little paranoid about being caught with expensive hardware purchases that won't cut the mustard now that we are in a new millenium. But, hey, in today's world, you can never be too certain, or too careful, when it comes to doubting anyone and everyone who has the least bit of contact along the road between you and your technology.

For instance, once, in 1997, I decided that, at my old age, I was going to prepare for some MCSE certification exams. For those of you aren't in the computer business, MCSE stands for Microsoft Certified Systems Engineer. To become one, you have to pass six exams covering four core subjects and two electives.

I didn't really plan to get MCSE certified, mind you. When you get really old, that's what you get to hire other people for. Studying, however, is one of those fun things to do to prove to yourself and those around you that you're not over the hill yet...like when former President Bush decided that his 70th decade wouldn't be complete without a jump from a flying airplane.

SYBEX Inc. publishes a marvelous study guide series for professional test takers, or others who want to carry around

Lesson 13... Talk is Cheap

very, very heavy textbooks and look really, really nerdy. I decided to start with the SYBEX "Windows® 95 Study Guide", since that is one of the tests and I figured I'm a Windows® professional: how hard can this stuff be?

When I got this bug up my nose, so to speak, to take an MCSE test a few years ago, I had not worked with Windows® 95 yet. But, having installed many a Windows® 3.11. network, with patches and bug fixes up through revision number 3211567.625499965, I wasn't worried.

I had seen plenty of action...even before "service packs" were invented. Service packs now replace bug fixes, which Microsoft declared no longer necessary and, besides, they are now illegal in the State of Washington, which is supported totally by the software industry.

So, I reasoned (again), how hard could this stuff be? My plan was to practice on my home made, Pentium 166, with 32 Mb RAM, learn all there was about the new easy Plug 'n Play operating system and then bring up an NT server at the office with Windows® 95 software clients. I'm a professional. Again, how hard could it be?

I suppose the marketing department of Microsoft had been hiring lots of focus group companies like Joe's for years, which is how they have been able to come to the conclusions that Windows® 95 is so much easier to install and use than the old 3.11.

The marketing department of Microsoft had also learned from these focus sessions, no doubt, that the best way to get its new operating system onto every possible computer made by every technology company that Microsoft doesn't own a part of (like Apple, for instance), is to get low-cost, NFR (Not For Resale) licensed copies into the hands of VARs (value added resellers) like me, for only $17.50.

Since the cost of the operating system is so low, they

SMART MARKETING

must have reasoned, and since these NFR copies are being sold to professionals, there's probably no reason to send the latest revisions with the latest bug fix...er service packs (Microsoft has declared that there are no such things a bug fixes). Surely, a focus group of VARs must have applauded wildly at the suggestion that they could get their hands on evaluation software two years after the release with all of the original eccentric frustrations.

And these NFR evals are not available on cheap to produce CD ROMs, mind you. They only came on older, harder to produce, more costly 3.5 diskettes. Diskettes have the endearing qualities of filling up embarrassingly empty bookshelves and they retain the rare, old charm of requiring six disks to change one driver.

I have to say, after the initial install, which provided four days of non-stop entertainment for less money than renting one of those "Honey, I Shrunk the (enter person or body part here) _____" movies, I couldn't possibly understand why anyone as busy as Janet Reno at the Justice Department would want to question the means and motives of Microsoft for knowing what's best for the world.

If I am such a smarty-pants professional, you may ask, how could it have taken so long to install one simple copy of Windows® 95? Good question. Firstly, there was the problem that my quality mouse, CD drive, printer and modem were no longer recognized after installing "plug-n-play". With some fabulous keyboard moves which I had learned back when men were men, women didn't smoke cigars and mice were for wimpy Mac users only, I was able to do some deep ini editing to get everything running but the modem.

Someone from Microsoft's free 90 day support line, which can be accessed within one hour, by anyone with a speakerphone and an automatic repeating dialer, spent almost two

Lesson 13... Talk is Cheap

hours leading me through keystrokes I cannot remember, except that, when we were through, my US Robotics modem still didn't work and my HP 855Cse printer no longer worked either.

After four more hours with two other people on that support line, I learned that neither US Robotics, nor Hewlett Packard, had 32 bit drivers, that it wasn't Microsoft's problem and that Microsoft could only be helpful when they control and manufacture all of the software, like they do with Microsoft Office 97. Now that's what I call great marketing. Are you listening, Ms. Reno?

Actually, I think that the Justice Department would prefer investigating the US Postal Service if they weren't fearful of being outmanned and outgunned. If you tick off Bill Gates, after all, what can he do to you, cancel your MSN account? The Post Office, on the other hand, can keep your mail in transit for years. Here's an example.

My good friend Howard Harris, Professor of Psychology and Chairman of the Human Services Department of Bronx Community College recently asked me to contribute a lesson on technology for a textbook he was completing.

I sent it via email to his AT&T account, but he never got it. I sent it again, but still nothing, so Howard sent me an email to verify his address. I replied back to his note, but he still got nothing, not from me, not from anybody. Howard complained to AT&T and within two weeks they were able to unclog the blockage with a big cyberplunger and they forwarded to him thirty two email messages that had been trapped in the ether.

In the meantime, I saved the lesson to diskette and stuck it in the mail. After all, if AOL could send thirty diskettes to every man, woman, child, dog, cat and hamster in America, I could send Howard one diskette.

Smart Marketing

The very next day, the diskette was delivered...to me. I brought it to the post office and spoke with the supervisor.

"This was delivered to me," I said.

"Fine," she said. "What's your problem?"

"It was delivered to me, the sender, here in Stamford, CT, not to the addressee in New York." I said.

"Oh, I'm sorry." she said. "I'll put your envelope into this big Official US Postal Service's envelope and I'll address it and send it right out. In a big US Postal Service's envelope, this diskette should get there in no time."

That's the problem with my trusting old ways. Joe, of Year 2000 letters, would have been smart enough to ask her exactly what the phrase "no time" really meant.

So, two weeks later, I got two calls. One was from Howard to tell me that AT&T had finally delivered the email, and one was from the supervisor at the local PO to say that my diskette had been returned marked no such person and no such address in Yonkers, NY.

"Is this the address you gave me?" the postal supervisor asked me.

"Almost," I replied.

We opened the envelope and took out my original one. The last digit of the zip code was one digit off.

"They could have found this," She said. "I'm surprised they didn't try. After all, it's in the same town and same post office and everything."

"Uh huh," I said.

Lesson 13... Talk is Cheap

The USPS, as it is fondly called down at the local rod and gun club, has been doing a lot of TV marketing to win our hearts, minds and packages. "Fed Ex, two-day, $11.00; UPS, two-day, $7.00; US Postal Service, two to three days, $3.00."

The slogan used to be "2 pounds, 2 dollars, 2 days," but the USPS found that they couldn't make money that way, nor could they make the two-day schedule. So, now I've heard people say that it's become "2 pounds, 3 dollars, 4 ever."

Suddenly all of that advertising money is down the mailing tubes because, like with any marketing program, your marketing will only work if you deliver the goods....eventually...like Microsoft's support center finally did on my fourth call to their fourth techie.

This guy knew a valuable, but undocumented secret, that Windows® 95 plug-n-play sometimes was unloading the much-needed MMSYSTEM.DLL in favor of older 16 bit Win 3.1 drivers. It's not a bug exactly; but aggravation like this is a good enough marketing reason for Microsoft to rethink its policy of releasing products that immediately require all those patches and service packs in order to work right.

After all this heartache, I read that Microsoft had announced a delay for its next new product. At that time it was NT 5.0. They would hold up shipping until fourth quarter '98. Finally, a product held until it worked. Sounded, to me, like a great start.

In some ways, this is not such a great marketing lesson. After all, Microsoft does pretty much own its market and so does the Postal Service. Marketing teaches us, however, to study trends. Can Microsoft stay on top without getting better at customer satisfaction and with Linux breathing down its neck? Can USPS, when UPS is doing such a great job?

Looking at it from the other side, both Linux and UPS can blast ahead, if the top dogs don't stay awake. If you are not the top dog, check and you'll see that your big competitor has weaknesses in customer service, poor product and distribution, etc. If you investigate these weaknesses, you will be able to do what Compaq did to IBM and what Dell did to Compaq… and, maybe, what Linux still may do to Microsoft.

LESSON FOURTEEN

The Devil's in the Details
·······

How I beat an extradition order and a fraud rap in Kentucky. It's amazing how a little mistake in a database can gum up your whole marketing day.

The other day, I received a telephone call from one of the national courier companies telling me that they were at my building address, but could not locate my office. Fact is, they were two blocks away from us, in our old office building. The sender company was sending us what was, evidently, to them, something important enough to pay overnight rates for, but not important enough for them to check where they were

SMART MARKETING

sending it. Boy, this must be important, I thought, sent by someone who hasn't been in touch with me for more than a year.

On another recent day, I received a telephone call from the receptionist of a Fortune 500 company, letting me know that an overnight delivery meant for me was delivered and signed for by someone in her mail room, along with the thirty or so other packages that were delivered. My package, addressed to their location, but to my attention, was sent overnight, important as the first example above, no doubt, equally unimportant enough to not check our address.

The devil is in the details, or, as we sometimes say, in the lack thereof. This is nothing new. Before Federal Express created the overnight delivery industry, before fax machines at reasonable cost created the "I must have it on my desk now" mentality, people still were creatively devising new ways to fools-rush to judgment, tarnishing their images faster than Superman can say, "Oh no! Not Kryptonite again!".

Back in 1982, I was hot on the lecture circuit, having just finished a book advising the hotel industry on how to take advantage of newly deregulated charges for hotel guest phone calls. At the time, I had been working for the American Hotel & Motel Association and one of my jobs was to convince FCC regulators that increasing the cost of phone calls, even above and beyond the cost of hotel rooms, was not, necessarily, a bad thing. It worked and, today, road warriors with dead batteries in their cell phones can add close to two hundred dollars worth of calls onto a bill for a $100 per night room.

Anyway, having just returned from an intellectually energizing conference of the Kentucky Hotel/Motel Association, where I had explained how to reap big bucks from telephone resale and hyped my book, I received a phone call from an admiring fan, advising me that I had just been indicted in Louisville and a warrant had been issued for my immediate arrest.

Lesson 14... The Devil's in the Details

"ARE YOU KIDDING?" I ASKED. "WHAT'S THEIR BUSINESS WHAT I DO IN THE PRIVACY OF MY OWN HOME?"

"NO. NOT THAT." THE CALLER SAID. "THEY'VE ISSUED THE WARRANT TO ARREST YOU FOR RUNNING A FLIMFLAM COMPUTER BUSINESS AND BILKING BIG BUCKS FROM US EASY-TO-FOOL, SIMPLE SOUTHERN BOYS.

"NOT ONLY THAT, BUT DAVID ARMSTRONG, THE JEFFERSON COUNTY COMMONWEALTH'S ATTORNEY HELD A PRESS CONFERENCE TODAY ANNOUNCING YOUR INDICTMENT AND EXTRADITION. IT WAS ON ALL THE TV STATIONS.

"YOU KNOW, WHEN YOU CAME DOWN HERE TO MAKE THAT SPEECH, YOU MADE THE LOCAL PAPERS. THEY RECOGNIZED THE NAME, FOUND A FEW MORE QUOTES OF YOURS IN THE *NEW YORK TIMES* AND TRACED YOU BACK HOME. NOW, THEY'RE FLYING UP TO NAB YOU."

Two days later, by Special Delivery Mail (1982 was before "absolutely, positively overnight," remember), I received copies of the Louisville papers.

Smart Marketing

From the *Louisville Courier Journal*:
Headline:
"Man allegedly bilked investors in his phony computer services."
Copy:
The magic word "computer" and a glib tongue enabled an alleged flimflam man to defraud local companies and individuals of $177,000, according to the Commonwealth's Attorney's Office. An indictment returned by the Jefferson County grand jury yesterday charged Stanley Rosenzweig, a former Louisville resident, with 13 counts of theft by deception over $100, two counts of theft by failure to make a required disposition of property, and one count of theft of services over $100.

From the *Louisville Times*:
Headline:
"Thousands allegedly taken in computer scheme."
Copy:
Stanley Rosenzweig lived in a sumptuous English Station home near the lush fairways of Midland Trail Golf Club and drove a shiny black Mercedes Benz convertible.

"He talked like he was the biggest thing to hit here since Muhammad Ali," says a neighbor. "But I guess it was just that - all talk."

One victim said, "A flimflam man like Mr. Rosenzweig, while some may believe his actions to be non-violent, reaps violent results on his

Lesson 14... The Devil's in the Details

VICTIMS...MY ONLY HOPE IS THAT THERE IS NOT AN-
OTHER VICTIM...THAT'S WHAT I'M FIGHTING FOR...IT'S
GOT TO BE STOPPED."

Wow, I thought. Warhol was right. I am finally getting my 15 minutes of fame. Their televised news conference was only fleeting, of course, but these news clippings I could keep in a scrapbook and use them in a marketing column. This is great, I thought. Unfortunately, my partner at the time had other ideas.

"YOU'VE GOT TO TELL THEM THEY'RE AFTER THE WRONG
ROSENZWEIG," HE SAID, "BEFORE THIS GETS OUT OF
HAND."

"WHY?" I PLEADED. "WHO WOULD BELIEVE THAT THERE ARE
TWO STANLEY ROSENZWEIG'S WHO GEEK AROUND
WITH COMPUTERS AND PHONES? BESIDES, THEY'LL
FIND OUT THEIR BIG MISTAKE WHEN THEY FLY ME DOWN
THERE AND FINGERPRINT ME, WON'T THEY?"

Maybe. Maybe not. So after enjoying five or six other phone calls from Kentucky hoteliers, who were, at the same time, concerned for my safety and curious about my alleged secret life, I finally picked up the phone and called the Commonwealth's Attorney.

Now, Jefferson County Commonwealth's Attorney David Armstrong was sort of like Special Prosecutor Kenneth Starr. Where there was an allegation of wrongdoing, he quickly had to decide:

1. If there was credible enough evidence that could be rammed through a grand jury for an indictment and
2. If the case was interesting enough to improve his political career.

Smart Marketing

Starr may, or may not, be interested in higher office, but Armstrong, it turned out, was campaigning at that very moment for higher State office, so any television coverage he got was OK by him.

I looked up Mr. Armstrong's phone number and dialed it.

"Hello," he said.

"Dave! Stan Rosenzweig from New York here. You don't know me from Adam. Why are you saying those nasty things about me? Isn't it possible that there is another guy with the same name?"

"Well, someone named Stan Rosenzweig did take a lot of money from innocent folks. Can you prove you're not him?"

"Sure Dave, I live in New York, spend a lot of time with Washington beaurocrats and have never lived in Kentucky. But, and you can correct me on this, aren't I supposed to be innocent until proved guilty by you? Shouldn't you be offering me proof that I AM this slug?"

"Well, that's true, but this is just the kind of conversation the flimflam Rosenzweig would try to pull on us. We're going to have to continue our course of action until we have evidence otherwise. Anything else you want to add?"

"Sure," I said. "I am no law enforcement expert, but it seems to me that if I were in your shoes, I might want to locate the rascal and slap the cuffs on him before I go blabbing at a TV press conference, don't you think? After all, if I were this guy, do you think I would be hanging

Lesson 14... The Devil's in the Details

AROUND A WHOLE WEEK WAITING FOR YOU TO SHOW UP?"

I won't thrill you with the rest of the conversation, except to report that Dave went out and held another press conference and told the press that I refused to cooperate. So, feeling the excitement of a fight like they now feel on Jerry Springer, I called the Louisville newspapers myself.

One reporter refused to print my side of the story but kept me on the phone for half an hour. I am sure he smelled a Pulitzer rising out of our conversation ("I'll keep him talking. You get the trace"). The other newspaper's reporter, younger, less career-minded and the more friendly of the two, reported my denial and actually checked the alleged details I allegedly provided.

What she allegedly, but easily, found out was that I had never lived in Kentucky, was ten years older then both the other Rosenzweig and Mr. Armstrong, and that I was shorter, heavier, and more hairless than them, too. These are actual details that were easily checked and could allegedly have saved Jefferson County time and money... not to mention Mr. Armstrong's alleged electoral career which has not gotten him to Washington, DC, but has gotten him to be the present day Mayor of Louisville. Sorry, Dave. Who knows where you might be today if only I had been the right Rosenzweig.

Two decades have gone by, since that case of mistaken identity, and it's as if all the new computing power in the world that we now have still will not help us when it comes to simple fact checking. We continue to get things wrong and we continue to lose consumer confidence, brand value, and real dollars.

If you would like to improve sales and profits, don't just threaten to fire the whole West Coast division. It may be time

Smart Marketing

to do a simple reality check to determine if all of your ammunition is accurate and is reaching your intended targets. Here is a simple questionnaire to help get you started:

1. Are your mailing lists accurate, or are you sending second and third mailings to the same wrong addresses as the first one?
2. Are your phone lists accurate, or are you wasting telemarketer time?
3. Are your client profiles up-to-date?
4. Does your database tell you which accounts are profitable and which are not, so you can spend more resources on the former and dump the latter?
5. Are you making critical marketing decisions based on valuable information, or are you just wasting everyone's time and money on programs that fail in the details?

Those two overnight packages that I mentioned at the beginning of this lesson turned out to be press releases from very well-known, high-priced public relations firms. Firstly, they wasted overnight fees by sending to the wrong place. Secondly, they wasted overnight fees by sending to the wrong person. Thirdly, for companies who make a living based on image, they came across looking really dumb.

Devilishly weak way to run a public relations firm, or any firm, for that matter. I allege that we all can do better.

Lesson 14... The Devil's in the Details

Armstrong was chasing the wrong Rosenzweig

By DOUG BEDELL
Louisville Times Staff Writer

It was too good to be true. And it wasn't.

When Jefferson County Commonwealth's Attorney David Armstrong held a press conference Wednesday to announce the indictment of Stanley Rosenzweig for allegedly swindling $177,000 from local investors and creditors, he had the notion that a New York Times article might lead to the arrest of the accused.

Holding up a copy of a July story from that newspaper's travel section, Armstrong said that a New York State resident called "Stanley Rosenzweig" was quoted prominently as an expert in "technology problems" of the hotel and motel industry.

The wanted Rosenzweig, before he left the Louisville area earlier this year, had allegedly represented himself as a technology whiz, expert in computers and typesetting. And Armstrong's office had information that he had moved to the New York City area.

An arrest seemed close-at-hand.

"Mr. Rosenzweig's present address is believed to be in New York State, and the necessary procedures to command his return to Kentucky are in the process of execution," Armstrong said in a news release.

But yesterday, the prosecutor reassessed the situation after getting a ation, for which the quoted Rosenzweig serves as a telecommunications consultant, said he has been a recognized bigwig in the field for years.

"I've never worked in Louisville, except last month I went down there and made a speech," he said. "Other than that, I have never had any gainful employment in Louisville — or ungainful for that matter."

When informed that The Courier-Journal, as well as television and radio news, had reported Armstrong's conclusion that he might be a swindler, the quoted Rosenzweig said he now understood why people had been acting so strangely toward him.

"I've had a lot of people calling me up and saying, 'Stan, your picture's in the paper!' and all kinds of stuff. And I say, 'Wait a minute! What's going on?'

"I've also had people come up and ask me, 'Did you ever own a computer company in Louisville?' I didn't know what was happening," he said.

Amused more than angry, Rosenzweig yesterday phoned Armstrong to complain. Armstrong was still skeptical. He had one of his investigators who knows the wanted Rosenzweig's voice listen to the conversation.

"I was just letting him talk, thinking that [the wanted] Rosenzweig is such a con artist that he'd try to con

LESSON FIFTEEN

Pricing as Marketing

How does creative pricing improve sales? Higher prices aren't always the most profitable.

Pricing is your engine lubricant. If margins are too thin to support your engine, sales volume will spin out of control without enough lubricating profits to support your sales engine. Without sufficient lubricating profit, your sales engine will soon self-destruct.

On the other hand, if margins are too thick, your engine may perform adequately on those warm, balmy days, but it will suffer the pains of sluggish turnover when the competitive days start to get dark and chilly. If margins, like engine lubricants, are too thick, on those really frosty competitive days, your sales engine may not crank at all.

In the old days, automobile owners were aware that different weights of oil were required for different seasons, but more recent advances in lubrication technology provides us with products that actually change weights at different temperatures to allow for less viscosity when it's freezing outside and heavier, more robust lubricating power when the engine heats up and really gets to humming.

In today's world of high tech, is your lubricating philosophy advanced enough to keep in step with the competitive temperature of the moment, or are you still inspecting the weight of your margins with each change of season, only a couple of times a year?

Walk down the aisle of any of the current popular discount "superstores" and you'll recognize the wide variance in profits from item to item. Some items, based on our knowledge of industry pricing, appear to be below-cost closeouts, while other hot products are priced with margins as high as 260%.

These stores vary margins from time to time to meet competition, or just to create traffic excitement and increase the sales tempo on slow days. Do you do that on an organized, planned and consistent basis? Is your profit lubricant multi-weight, multi-temperature rated?

The more miles you go in your car, the less you have to change your oil and, thus, long steady drives are less demanding on your lubricant and on your engine. In sales, too, you can profit from lower margins from long, steady client relationships, while short-term customers and projects with small dollar values may require higher margins, or may not be worthwhile at any price.

That's why a quart of oil costs as little as 99 cents at the discount variety store where you may be plunking down 60 bucks on other purchases, and costs two dollars a quart at the gas station where the total profit on the sale may be less.

I have often quoted renowned sailboat designer Bruce Kirby who told me that the ability to win races is directly tied

Lesson 15... Pricing as Marketing

to your ability to sense approaching changes in wind and waves and to shift gears ahead of the pack. In other sports, too, flexibility, and the ability to adapt and change mid-course, separates winners from losers.

We don't win by consistently earning the highest percentage of profits per order. That was the lesson of Ivory Tower Business School. We win by earning the greatest amount of after-cost profit dollars. Highest profit dollars come from adding in the cost of time and trouble when we make a true value-added sale and taking out that value-added multiple when we are simply moving boxes. That is the lesson of the street.

LESSON SIXTEEN

Getting the Job Done Through People...and Printing

> How to integrate collateral materials and people wisely. Of all the means available to take your products to market, here are a few practical tips before you pay the printer.

Well-publicized morale problems at the U.S. Postal Service and Gun Club have got me to thinking about the role of leadership in management. Management leadership is defined as "getting the job done through people". In successful companies, it is a concept based on respect for people and understanding of the job. The definition of management is strictly results oriented.

Smart Marketing

Unfortunately, when inexperienced managers establish expectations without the benefit of trying out their ideas down on the playing field themselves, they soon find that the people they were counting on don't produce quite as expected. These managers find that they don't make their quarterly numbers and then, eventually, they find the door...as it should be.

Now most of us who develop marketing programs know that, to make them work, we need to manage field troops to sell for us. We do this, usually, in two ways:

- We hire them, train them, pay them, take all the risk, and send them out to represent us. We employ them, and/or
- We don't employ them, but sign up dealers, let them share the startup risk and offer greater profit potential at the back end.

I have heard many aspiring sales managers say that it is not possible to attract talent using the second method. Others say that the only way to assure success is to find entrepreneurial souls who take risks for big rewards. We can look within our industry to the vast independent consulting network, and outside of our industry to industries like insurance to see that the second method does work, if we closely manage both our sales and our marketing efforts.

One of the most successful companies using the second method is Mary Kay Cosmetics. Mary Kay has given thousands of women who also juggle complex homemaking responsibilities, the opportunity to rake in six figure incomes...and they do.

Mary Kay has learned that, to do this, one should never boss sales people, but one must manage them instead by providing the marketing support we would expect if we were in the field. One must "get the job done through people".

Lesson 16... *Getting the Job Done Through People...and Printing*

Indeed, I was quite moved, at a sales and marketing conference, when Mary Kay's then Vice Chairman Richard C. Bartlett told his audience that he considered every single one of the firm's thousands of dealers to be his boss...and he meant it, too. This executive had transcended the business battle of the sexes to find great financial success by thinking of himself as being bossed by ten thousand housewives (and the rest of us men can't even put our socks in the hamper and take out the trash without feeling a sense of accomplishment).

The management at Mary Kay has learned that, even when we go the dealer route, we need to set corporate direction through product differentiation, positioning and collateral materials. Mary Kay doesn't pay money to its independent agents for anything but a sale, but it provides a top-quality family of products, superior sales training and marketing materials that everyone is very proud of.

It is here at the collateral materials level that many of us fail the test miserably, because we don't grasp the basic concept of thinking like our dealers - the guys in the street. As a result, we build our materials in a vacuum and a vacuum, as it turns out, sucks dirt.

Here's an example. A client of ours distributes products for a larger reseller. He showed me a beautifully printed brochure that the reseller had obviously spent a bundle on.

"THIS LOOKS GREAT," I SAID. "I'LL BET YOU CAN SURE MAKE MONEY WITH THIS."

"NOPE," CAME THE REPLY. "THE BROCHURE LOOKS GOOD, BUT THE PRODUCT IS NEITHER LOWER IN PRICE, NOR HIGHER IN QUALITY THAN OTHER SIMILAR PRODUCTS. THERE'S NOTHING TO MAKE IT SPECIAL. MOREOVER, THESE GUYS PUT THEIR OWN 800 NUMBER ALL OVER THIS THING. HOW CAN I GIVE THESE OUT WITHOUT

SMART MARKETING

HAVING THEM GIVE THE RESULTING LEADS TO MY COMPETITION?"

Good point, I thought. Here is a case where the reseller either didn't think about his channel dealers, or didn't care about them, or the big reseller had an alternative agenda that didn't include them in future plans. "Why don't I test them out for you?" I volunteered, and I did just that.

I called the 800 number on those fancy brochures and got a receptionist who had no sales training whatsoever. She passed me to a rep who put me on hold for four minutes (It's my business to keep track of these things) and then someone took my name and number. She didn't ask me where I got the brochure, or if I knew anybody who sold this product.

Thus, my client was right; the brochure was of little use to him. He lost, because his supplier had only a sophomoric understanding of the dynamics of marketing, didn't have a unique product niche and didn't provide the support for his dealer to sell successfully.

The supplier lost, big time, because, by failing to produce a differentiated product and collateral materials that support his dealers, he forfeited his right to this most valuable of resources: people. The supplier has failed the management leadership role to "get the job done through people". Why? Because he didn't think enough of his dealers to ask them.

The failure to do adequate marketing research among our own strategic partners hurts more struggling and aspiring companies than the economy, competition, or global warming. Nothing sells for us like preparation. We all know this. So how come we continue to shoot from the lip and run with every new costly idea before we test it out with our market partners?

Any sales campaign, brochure, advertisement, new product introduction, SPIF, option, limited time offer, gift, or

Lesson 16... Getting the Job Done Through People...and Printing

positioning change without field investigation is nothing more than a bad idea gone worse. Blame your poor sales on the Republicans, or the Democrats, if you will, but the real problem is often you, because, in the words of my Aunt Mabel who never flinched when asking people how much money they were making, "If you don't ask, you don't know."

The next time you decide to roll out something new, be it product, or marketing material, ask yourself these penetrating questions:

- Who really needs this? How do I know? Who will buy it? Why do they want to change from what they have?
- Who will sell this? Is it really what the field sales people need to have in their bag of tricks? How do they feel about it? Will they respond to this by outselling my projections two to one, or will they merely thank me politely and put it on the shelf 'til it turns yellow at the edges?
- What is it about this idea that I don't know, because I was too impetuous or egotistical to find out before I plunked down my hard earned bucks on a roll out?

Remember, the people who choose to take your message to the streets and the materials you choose to have them carry are so very, very closely intertwined, and that to consider one without the other is often almost as damaging as not taking any action at all. Incomplete data often results in faulty conclusions. Here's a case in point.

The *New York Times* once reported that during 1991 there were 5,771 pedestrians killed by automobiles in the U.S. In these accidents, 16.9% of the drivers were intoxicated, while

Smart Marketing

32.7% of the victims were drunk. Twice as many drunk victims as drunk drivers. Conclusion: we have a significant drunk walking problem in our country.

Does this mean that, statistically, you should let the poor souse drive home so his odds will be better? Of course not. The incomplete data doesn't take into account that our drunk friend, behind the wheel, may kill, not only pedestrians, but other motorists, and even himself. Further study would tend to indicate that you still should take away your friend's car keys if he is drunk...but, maybe you need to take his shoes, as well.

In <u>Smart Selling</u>, Lesson Nineteen, I cautioned you to beware the "ides" of marketing... unfinished ideas that hurt rather than help because they are costly in both time and money, and they take us down the wrong track, killing our existing momentum, resulting in fewer sales, not more. Few ideas are as unfinished as those that fail to include the thoughts of the eyes and ears of our sales agents and resellers.

LESSON SEVENTEEN

Charging for Support

What part of your service is proprietary and worth more? Unbundling services can improve your year end bottom line. Here's how.

Charging for service, what a novel concept. Do you provide a real proprietary value added product? (And by proprietary I mean that it is only available from you.) If you do, you can cut your margin to ribbons in order to get the sale and you'll still make money by building a great repeat business with excellent profits, based on servicing what you have sold.

On the other hand, if you only sell generic, non-proprietary, shrink wrapped, commodity products (the kind that everyone else sells), then, even though there is strong price pressure to abandon your margins, you will not be able to depend on

Smart Marketing

service revenues, because you will be fighting the margin battle for non-proprietary services after the initial sale, too.

In other words, if you have something special to offer, you'll make a good living, but, if you don't, you might as well call the undertaker...you're as good as dead.

Often, we all find ourselves at a major marketing crossroads. Do we try to charge enough for our applications, hardware, software and installations to make a modest profit and continue to provide free service for some specific period of time? Or, do we give the stuff away at bargain basement prices, hoping to get our prospects permanently wedded to us so we can sell high profit service contracts later?

Back in the late 70's and early 80's, when I owned a telephone systems (interconnect) company, we began facing increasingly stiffer competition from hungrier telephone equipment vendors who would cut margins to unbelievably low levels. This was back when discounting was king and a deep discounting home appliance seller named Crazy Eddie was an icon to be worshipped. Crazy Eddie sold for less than his costs, figuring to make it up in volume, sort of like the dot com companies of recent days. And, just like these more recent dot coms, Eddie ran out of money just about when Wall Street got tired of his losses. I can't remember the details, except that the company disappeared and Eddie ended up in jail.

We didn't subscribe to the red ink model and we tried telling prospects that service after the sale was more important than purchase price. Yeah! Like they really believed that one.

Well, for a while it looked like they were starting to believe it, but then a company called Teletronics started giving away two years free service... then three years free service... then FIVE years.

Customers flocked to the low prices and free support. One prospect told me he couldn't resist and that it was too

Lesson 17... Charging for Support

good to be true. He was right. It WAS too good. They went bust... just like Crazy Eddie. We hadn't sold at a loss and we did not go bust.

The smart thing we did was go back to those orphan accounts and sell them service contracts. The dumb thing we did was not keep a good database of who all those accounts were. Of course, if you remember the state of computing 20 years ago...well, we didn't know what a database was. In fact, we didn't even own our first computer until 1978, and it was only used for word processing until 1983.

Today, there is a conceptual battle going on regarding the value added pricing of service versus the future value of a captive, or semi-captive customers. When Corel and Red Hat sell for less than cost, thousands of copies of Linux and associated applications like WordPerfect software, they are betting that by buying the market they can create an after market in software and services that will eclipse their current product publishing costs.

When Amazon.com and Snap.com spend more per individual web visitor than they can earn from their purchases, they are assuming that, somewhere down the road, these visitors will provide a back end cash flow. This business plan requires high-dollar profits at some point... and high profits can best be assured by bringing in as many jobs as possible and building a steady, ongoing, recurring revenue stream of after sale services. Will it ever work for dot coms with a loss-leader mind set? Who knows.

In our case, eventually, we decided to increase our repeat service business by expanding our market into newer technology PC based voice mail systems that our competitors were unfamiliar and uncomfortable with. For a while, we were able to sell at good margins and still provide great benefits to our customers. Then some companies started repeating the low margin

Smart Marketing

and free service offers of our nemesis of the '70's, Teletronics and it was "*deja vu* all over again," as Yogi would say.

One competitor went so far as to offer a major Connecticut publisher a technically obsolete phone system and an associated voice mail system for less money than dealer cost on a stand alone voice mail. Publishers are not paid to be technically sophisticated, so how can they know the difference? It's not easy.

We countered this low-ball threat by adding in an almost unlimited array of feature growth.

Thus, we kept adding new features to keep adding to the added value of ongoing service revenues for our products and services. We saved our clients new money every day, so that it served them well to stay tied to us.

What we gained from this experience is that you can continue to sell sophistication with marginal markups by building substantial ongoing proprietary support that produces an ongoing revenue stream. That is what your accountant does. The customer benefits are:

- useable operating improvements,
- genuine cost savings,
- consistently good service,
- improved image, and
- better service to the customers of your customers.

With a little thought, you may be able to modify your initial margins, increase your service base and become so valuable to your accounts that they must stay with you forever. This is preferable to the occasional high profit killer sale which has no after-sale revenue stream and creates no ongoing value to your franchise.

LESSON EIGHTEEN

Adding Value to Commodities
. . . . . .

Don't fool yourself into believing that you add value. How to separate the real value from the commodity.

    Adding value to commodity selling...and other bull stories. I've been shaking my head in disbelief at the stuff I've been reading lately about how to improve margins by talking up the same old story of added services we provide.

    Like we don't already try that...and like it hasn't become so much of a tired cliche to our prospects. One friend and customer confided that if another salesman tries to sell him a competitive commodity product at a higher price "because of our commitment to service", he's going to deck him.

    Let's face it, Ivory Tower guys, that selling concept is stone cold, so go out and bury it. If you're not in the trenches and you don't already know that, you're officially over the hill. So stop preaching textbook selling. It doesn't work anymore, because the American consumer, both at home and at the office, is tuned to a new paradigm: product similarity.

Smart Marketing

I just reread a terrific article from *Barron's Financial Weekly* that cited, among other things, that Phillip Morris and other big food companies are not such good investments any more (Phillip Morris, as you may know, saw the finger of death's handwriting on the wall a few year's back and diversified from tobacco to food by buying both General Foods AND Kraft).

The *Barron's* article said, in effect, that the statistics favoring the migration from brand name to store brand-generic is a rapidly growing snowball that has a lot of hill left to roll over. To paraphrase, once they try supermarket brand Corn Flakes and wake up the next morning to find that they haven't died of it, it will be very hard to get them to go back to Kellogg's.

This is a tough blow to cigarette/food companies, because they have already lost the brand name loyalty of smokers, 68% of those who live will now defect to another brand in any one year.

Often, in the case of foods, many of us believe that the brand name and generic products flow from the same factory, although, in reality, we don't really know, or care. That's the concept of product similarity.

Here are some of those similar products that have merged in our minds to become, for many Americans, easily and functionally interchangeable, where neither is perceived to be worth spending more for than the other: FedEx or UPS; AT&T, Worldcom or SPRINT; American Airlines or Continental; gas heat or oil heat; Lean Cuisine or Weight Watchers frozen meals; New York or LA.

In our business, perceived product similarity means that if your company hasn't standardized on Windows 2000 or Linux, then either can meet your needs.

More and more customers are buying deeply discounted and generic brands from their favorite new website without

Lesson 18... Adding Value to Commodities

major incident. This is causing fits in the brick and mortar sector, but is this all bad?

It is bad only if you ask those merchandising dinosaurs who were too slow to adapt. You can put up roadblocks to the future or you can get on the information highway. When you get right down to it, some of the more established businesses sound just like the bloated hospitals and pharmaceutical companies that massed their armies responding to Hillary Clinton's health care proposals. They won, but not for long. You can't legislate against progress.

All of this product similarity thinking isn't very bad if you ask anyone who has been smart enough and quick enough to understand these trends and switch gears to meet the market. Dell's sales and profits are up each and every year. In fact, lots of folks have stars that are on the ascent. Have you asked yourself why some seem to soar with the economy, while most of the public companies on the New York and Nasdaq exchanges are hurting badly?

Several years ago, I interviewed Bruce Kirby, internationally acclaimed boat designer (Americas Cup and smaller racing class boats), and asked him how he managed to win in a field of 45 competitors in an annual regatta of a boat class that he had designed.

> "YOU HAVE TO BE SENSITIVE TO THE WIND AND THE WAVES AND BE READY TO SWITCH GEARS AT ANY MOMENT," HE SAID. "IF YOU CAN'T DO THAT, YOU CAN'T COMPETE."

It's amazing how many of us can't switch gears and are left stalled at the light. I fell a little behind getting this Lesson finished, because, as part of my regular job, I spent the better part of the week interviewing candidates for a sales manager's position.

Smart Marketing

Applicants to our small company include former VPs of huge corporations who have been merged, downsized or early retired out of a job. They all talk of value-added selling, of upgrading profitability of the sale, of hiring support staff to formalize presentations, of large salaries, and of benefits...to them, not to us.

One ex-IBMer prepared a budget for his new department that looked so inviting, I thought about applying for the job myself. I have learned, from this, the real life difference between running a big-budget corporate department (other people's money) and running a pay-as-you-go, entrepreneurial department (your own money). In our world, if it doesn't show an immediate payout, or a clear path to one, we don't do it.

If you have a way to go public and can make your retirement nest egg from selling stock in your cash hemorrhaging company, that's the Amazon.com business model and who is to say that it won't turn around, eventually. If, on the other hand, you don't have access to the public trough and you want to build a business based on real earnings, then you must heed the advice of famed boat designer and racer Bruce Kirby and be nimble enough to "switch gears" as soon as and as often as the "weather conditions" around you change.

That could be why Phillip Morris is where it is today and why Xerox is where it is. And this, finally, brings us to the crux of the matter. How do we learn to shift gears today? What is the great secret shift pattern? Here are the answers to both questions.

Lesson 18... Adding Value to Commodities

Firstly, if you can't make money on a commodity product, don't sell it, support it. We used to sell a fair amount of a popular contact management software until the manufacturer stole one of our customers.

After that, we dumped our inventory and focused on the three things that every customer wants. They say the three most important things in real estate are: location, location and location. Well the three most important things in data management are: get it to work, get it to work, get it to work.

If you sell someone a FAX board, a laser printer or a copy of Microsoft SQL server, they think that they bought your good will, knowledge and support until the second coming of David Koresh (remember him?). But if you let them buy those things from Discount Louie, they'll give you their home, car and first born to make them work as designed.

So my advice for adding value to commodity products is that you should totally unbundle all commodities. Tell your customers that you can't spend the rest of your life supporting a laser printer that you sold at a $30 margin (or whatever it is that you now sell at practically no margin), but that you will be happy to sell them a fairly priced, hand-holding service contract no matter where they buy their commodities.

In our office technology arena, internet access is an incredible commodity opportunity to help customers, yourself and mankind. Forget about 56k slowpokes. Everyone is now pushing the envelope on throughput to over 1 megabit and the new DSL, cable and wireless standards promises to multiply that by ten. You'll soon be able to send entire laser disks of information via email in the time we used to send quick three line messages, dropping delivery costs, well, to zip. But service and maintenance is not only restricted to cyberspace. Service profit is not even restricted to products that break a lot.

When I was in the telephone installation and mainte-

Smart Marketing

nance business, we sold a terrific systems product that rarely needed service. Still, we needed to keep trucks, parts and people on call round the clock, even on weekends, just in case. This wasn't a cheap stand-by service for us to provide.

Often, our customers didn't want to pay for service on an annual contract basis after the first year, because they never saw a repair truck and couldn't see the hidden cost unless we pointed it out to them. They all bought our "phantom service". Why? Because we explained that it was in their best interest to have those trucks rolling, whether they needed them or not.

Consider this. Most businesses will never have a fire or flood. Not only will they not need fire insurance, but they won't even need a fire department. Most owners will never need disability coverage and might not even need major medical insurance. I, for one, have always felt pretty healthy.

We didn't sell only service. We sold service CAPA-BILITY, the pre-purchased ability to respond to emergencies if and when they occur...and we sold them in four tiers:

1. Full parts and labor any time you call.
2. Full labor during business hours and parts at 25% off.
3. Priority call at 50% of regular labor rate and discounted parts.

Lesson 18... Adding Value to Commodities

4. Don't pay us if you don't need us, but we won't come until we have solved every problem of every customer who has paid to keep our "firehouse" open.

That concept works well in today's environment of product similarity, regardless of the particular commodity in your business. If you sell anything that is shrink-wrapped, off the shelf, or prepackaged by someone else, and you want to differentiate yourself from the competition, then differentiate yourself from those products.

Establish distance. Separate yourself from the commodity and you will be able to set your price for your time irrespective of the price, or the markup, of the commodity in question. Establish your rate (hourly, weekly, annually, per incident, etc.) at the start of each business relationship and you will always have cash flow from your time expended. Then, regardless of how often the wind shifts, you will always be a winner.

LESSON NINETEEN

Greater Wealth Through Smart Positioning
. . . . . .

Redefine your market by developing new products and services to sell to your existing customer base. Four steps to reposition your way to success and a three step plan to roll it out.

Here are four ways to get rich (or even richer, if you already have a bundle). You can define a new niche and increase sales to new accounts, you can redefine your market by developing new products and services to sell to your existing customer base, you can reposition your price points by reducing expenses, or you can marry somebody very, very wealthy.

At first glance, these methods sound a lot like sales strategies, but, in fact, all four of them, have to do with the marketing concept called positioning, or repositioning, which is the ability to get your prospects to see you in a very particular

SMART MARKETING

(and desirable) light, with the result being that they give you their money. It has worked for me. It will work for you. Shucks, repositioning has been profitable for just about everybody, including Woody Allen, Pee Wee Herman and Bill Clinton.

For instance, in this current environment of kinder, gentler, shrinking margins, we can still take a positioning lesson from FedEx. Positioning its air courier service as the one to call "when it absolutely, positively has to be there overnight", FedEx did a great job of defining itself into a great growth explosion even when the business world was crumbling all around it. As a result, for years we wouldn't even think of calling anyone else. By positioning itself as the consummate reliable courier, it was all but impossible for anyone to compete by offering something so crass as a lower price.

UPS, however, was able to effect a major competitive positioning assault after it recognized that its own slightly lower pricing wasn't enough of a reason for the rest of us to trust our vital packages to it. It redefined its strategy that reliable service and better management was its true source of power, which resulted in UPS being able to offer lower prices. Thus the UPS positioning slogan, "We run the tightest ship in the shipping business" was a comfortable rationale for the lower prices it offers and we seek. UPS has turned cost reduction into more than a profit enhancer, it has turned it into an enviable marketing concept. Now FedEx absolutely, positively, needs to come up with new material.

Positioning has helped to make Microsoft the company it is today. When DOS became the standard for PCs, Bill Gates won a gold medal in the software Olympics. He could have retired right then and there like Olympic swimming star Mark Spitz, and others, who flashed momentary brilliance, then faded into oblivion. But was billion-dollar megawealth enough for Gates? Of course not. He had a company to reposition. To

Lesson 19... Greater Wealth Through Smart Positioning

Gates, the growth of the PC market meant that there was now a hoard of existing customers to sell new stuff to... a window of opportunity, if you will... and now, the folks at IBM, Apple and, yes even AOL, view the imagination of Bill Gates with the same reverence and fear that you and I have reserved for Stephen King.

If you really want to learn how to reposition your business, take a lesson from the insurance industry. Insurance people know that you and I would rather have our heirs and beneficiaries come into their inheritances prematurely than for us to spend another exciting hour with our insurance agent. But wait! This is now the 21st century and, today, through the miracle of positioning, you hardly hear from insurance agents anymore. Instead, you get calls from Mutual of Whatever's Registered Financial Planner who will be happy to help you with your investment portfolio, insurance and all.

Positioning is the watchword of the insurance business. I recently visited with a regional sales manager for the National Association for the Self Employed, which is an insurance company that let's just say has been well positioned. NASE has an incredible 68-page catalog of services, all in full color and on glossy stock. The book explains all that NASE does for you, from lobbying in Washington for the little guy, to discounts on magazine subscriptions to *Business Week*, *Forbes* and *Entrepreneurial Woman*.

But much of this may only be a clever disguise, not only for being in the insurance business, but for being in insurance multi-marketing. For those who have been living in caves, multi-marketing is the concept where one person sells something at an enormous markup and a dozen people up the chain earn enough to pay the rent.

Newspapers in principal cities are running classified sales ads offering HUGE incomes from NASE "managers" looking to increase their downline action. Applicants are treated to a 40-minute videotape of sales awards, trips, bonuses, overrides and commissions. All for signing up association members? Not quite. The big bucks are reserved for those agents who sign up individual entrepreneurs for hospital and medical benefits insurance that is sold as association benefits.

Am I suggesting that you turn your business into a pyramid game? No. But I am suggesting that if you take a hard look at the lessons that those in other industries have learned about what moves our markets so that we, too, can work smarter instead of harder. After all, if a cigarette company can turn a smelly, ugly, camel into a Pied Piper of pre-teens, imagine what you and I could do with a laptop, tactile rollerball.

Here are four steps to repositioning your way to success and riches:

1. **Define your objectives.**

This is basic. This is boring. This is in every Management 101 text, Chapter 1. This is critical. You can't decide what road you want to take until you decide where you want to be. Be realistic, though, and make sure that your objectives are in line with your added value. Back when Saddam decided that he wanted to be in Kuwait, he had set his objectives, but his research didn't reflect the ideas of the rest of the world as to his added value. Saddam might have been more successful if he had read the other three steps.

2. **Focus, focus, focus. Research, research, research.**

Learn from your customers. Learn from your prospects.

Lesson 19... *Greater Wealth Through Smart Positioning*

Learn from your suppliers. You can even learn from history and politics.

Democratic Party focus groups have been studying focus reports and they have determined that, deep down inside, Americans are not happy about losing Social Security, or paying high taxes, or paying high energy costs, or not having better schools and teachers. Thus the most recent democratic campaign (as of this printing) has positioned Al Gore as our key to economic and educational salvation.

Republican focus groups, in stiff competition, came to the same conclusions as the Dems... that life is good, but that we need to be mindful of the future in education and social Security.

Much like the UPS assault on Federal Express, the Bush folks and the Gore folks battle for our perceptions using ammunition in the form of research from the field. Today, this is what we all must have in order to make the right strategic decisions. Not only must we gather information, but we must use that information to redefine ourselves and/or our products effectively.

What if you found out that most prospects couldn't care less about the genius of your product, because it doesn't really help them improve their business, or profits, or life, etc.? Would you stay with it anyway, the way a Captain stays with his sinking ship? Well, I have a news flash for you. Nobody has gone down with the ship in years, except maybe those hardy Ph.D. folks at Long Term Capital.

The lesson for today is: if the ship doesn't float, GET OFF. Use your new research to redefine your product, or get a whole new product, if you have to, but don't waste your time trying to sell something after you've determined that it doesn't have a market.

Smart Marketing

3. **Write a mission statement identifying the real added value of what you do.**

In an informal poll I took of 32 company owners who read my column and were generating less that $1 million per year in sales, only five could come up with a succinct response to identify his core value that would convince anyone else but his mother.

Let's face it, if you don't know what value you add to the game, you're not really in the game. Of the twenty-seven in my poll who failed (yes, failed) this test, some said that they had proprietary software that met certain industry needs. All said that they had years of systems experience that made them uniquely qualified. Uniquely qualified?

Do you know what unique means? Rare, single, uncommon, unusual, walks to the beat of a different drummer! Can the 27 out of 32 who had no other distinguishing features all be unique? Like I said, maybe to mom. If you want to convince your prospects, if you even want to HAVE prospects, try defining the value you provide. You cannot move ahead until you do.

Lesson 19... *Greater Wealth Through Smart Positioning*

4. Build a campaign plan.

Presidential races, Gulf wars and marketing strategies are called campaigns. They are crusades, battles joined, tactics and procedures established, maneuvers planned and executed, all with a single goal in mind: Attain your stated objective.

Your campaign can have more subplots than the X Files, if you wish, or it can be as simple as A, B, C. Here's a sample of A, B, C:

A. Create a defining image of your campaign theme through a logo, a slogan or a jingle.

Well recognized examples include "tightest ship in the shipping business", "Miller Time", "Intel Inside", "When you care enough to send the very best", "I'll take it", "Be all that you can be". How about a well-defined company name that says it all like "www.buy.com"?

Former President Bush was consistently creative in using effective campaign slogans such as "Family values", "Read

Smart Marketing

my lips", "A thousand points of light", "Tax and spend democrats". These word pictures do end-runs around our logic centers and cut straight to our emotional decision-maker circuits. They are the very essence of positioning. Lee Iacocca's "Buy American" campaign was extremely successful in turning around an almost bankrupt car company, which hurt the major importers like Toyota, Nissan and now, of course, Daimler-Chrysler.

B. Prepare direct mail, print ads and telemarketing based on your newly created theme.

Identify lists of prospective and existing customers. Test it on a limited audience, say about 100 prospects, and then refine the material. Train your selling staff, if you have one, so that everyone understands the company's mission, product, strategy and objectives.

C. Turn 'em loose, and "go for the gusto!"

Hit the streets with the new company position in print, mail, phone and live presentations. Keep tight control and track results so that you can make adjustments. Buy a bigger cash register.

Our campaigns are similar to A, B, C, and follow the well-known KISS formula. At least, I used to think that it was a well-known formula. Once when I was nearing the end of a training talk, I asked the group if they knew what the KISS formula meant. Dozens of hands went up, of course, but one hand was shaking violently, like that of a third-grader who urgently needed the pass to the toilet.

"ALL RIGHT," I SAID, CALLING ON THIS HAND THAT WOULDN'T BE DENIED. "WHAT DOES KISS MEAN."

Lesson 19... Greater Wealth Through Smart Positioning

"After spending all day tied to this chair, I think it means, Kan I Still Sell?" He said.

There are times to plan, and times to fight and times to call it a day. Knowing when to do each is the true mark of leadership.

"Of course it does," I said. "Meeting adjourned."

LESSON TWENTY

Seven Creative Ways to Reach Your Marketing Objectives Without Paying an Arm and a Leg
......

>These seven promotions are easy to accomplish, are low in cost, and just as important, they are charitable. They improve your brand image in the community and increase sales.

    *I*n summary, they are: 1. Give away the store. 2. Sponsor a school essay contest. 3. Newsletter delights. 4. Linkage. 5. The greater glory promotion. 6. The altruistic seminar. 7. The turkey trot.

    Ever notice how October sneaks up on you before you are anywhere near meeting the year's sales goals? When you

SMART MARKETING ——

have only eight more weeks 'til Christmas, and if you hope to have enough pocket cash do any holiday shopping, you need a fast-track program to get those last-minute end-of-year orders in...RIGHT NOW!

For three SUPER autumn marketing projects, then I suggest you go down to the super-market and gobble up all of their turkeys. I promise you that the result will give you a yummy fourth quarter, a stuffed checkbook, and a proud ego that will make you as smug as me.

We resellers don't like to think of ourselves as being as crassly commercial as retailers and you and I can probably think of a dozen reasons NOT to give away plump Thanksgiving turkeys. Turkey inventory needs cold storage and could pose a health risks, right? And besides, if birds of a feather flock together, will those of us who run Thanksgiving turkey promotions end up looking like, uh, turkeys? Hopefully not.

On the other hand, there are lots of good reasons for a "free Thanksgiving turkey" promotion. For one thing, it's hard to find anybody who doesn't enjoy a FREE Thanksgiving turkey, including every one of your prospects.

Secondly, this is not an expensive, or complicated way to market your business, since turkeys are about 39 cents a pound in November, or about $8.00 per 20-lb. bird. This is a very inexpensive way to be remembered.

Thirdly, turkeys are larger than life. You can't tell me that prospects who spend Thanksgiving with their families chowing down YOUR dinner won't remember you fondly through the next decade. Years from now they'll say,

> "REMEMBER WHEN WE ALL GOT TOGETHER TO EAT THAT SOFTWARE GUY'S TURKEY? BOY THAT BIRD WAS GOOD...AND THE LEFTOVERS LASTED THE ENTIRE WEEK. WHAT A SHAME COUSIN FLOYD CHOKED ON A BONE

Lesson 20... Seven Creative Ways to Reach Your Marketing Objectives

AND HAD TO BE RUSHED TO THE HOSPITAL BEFORE WE SERVED AUNT MARTHA'S PUMPKIN PIE. OH, WELL. THE PIE SURE WAS GOOD, TOO."

Fourthly, you can use the occasion to do some good for your community and reap personal and professional rewards for your trouble.

Here are three altruistic ways to carry yourselves to success on turkey wings (which are certainly more substantial and taste better these days than gossamer wings).

Plan One: Feed the homeless

Offer a second free turkey to a local homeless shelter, the Salvation Army, or other responsible group that ministers to the hunger of local people who are less fortunate. Of course, this is in addition to the free turkey to the prospects who sign up with you on or before Thanksgiving Day (or Christmas, or New Year's). If this proves successful, you might have to send a dozen turkeys to that shelter, which should turn into a media event if you have been taking the press relations advice that was covered in Lesson Four.

So pick up the phone right now and call your local super market chain to work out a co-sponsorship arrangement, exchanging promotional considerations for discounts and for inventory cold storage. You might also consider talking to a local restaurant owner about cooking that huge Thanksgiving dinner and sharing in the credit.

For your prospects who are fence sitters, this is a way to get them off that fence and into the spirit of the season, to do some community good and to grace more than their family tables when they place that order that you know (hope) is coming sooner or later anyway. For prospects who don't eat turkey, don't care about the homeless and continue to sit on that un-

Smart Marketing

comfortable fence, maybe you should send them holiday tubes of Preparation H.

Plan Two: Not much different from Plan One, except maybe you would like to send some of that food (or an equivalent check through the Red Cross) to people just like you and me, hard working folks, who, thanks to the Hurricane of the Month, haven't a prayer for getting back into their homes by Thanksgiving.

Not that the local homeless aren't just as needy...In fact, think of the promotional effects of your being big hearted enough to do BOTH of these relatively inexpensive promotions, not to mention how good it will feel.

Plan Three: The good old fashioned Thanksgiving turkey trot - Sponsor a Thanksgiving day race through your local Road Runners Club, YMCA, YWCA or other fitness organization.

Keep the race short, about a 5k (3.1 miles), or have 5k and 10k divisions to get more participation. Turkeys to the winners. For greater fun and interest, require runners to carry a pumpkin (some pumpkins are the size of tennis balls), a gourd, or a piece of Indian corn...or have every runner wear Pilgrim style hats, etc. You get the idea. The prizes are turkeys, of course,.

Remember to invite ALL of your clients and prospects...even those who are in other parts of the country. It doesn't hurt to let them know that you are involved in the community.

Here's the administration:

Call your newspaper, your Chamber of Commerce, the editors of the newsletter or magazines of the vertical market you serve. Let them know that you are running this public ser-

Lesson 20... Seven Creative Ways to Reach Your Marketing Objectives

vice event and ask them to cover it. If they can't, ask them how you can provide the information in a form that they can use.

DON'T RELY ON PRESS RELEASES. These can get lost. Be sure to have a direct conversation with the editorial decision-makers. Then follow up with a written account of your promotion.

Call your hottest prospects and your favorite customers and send them copies of the written press material. Ask your prospects if they would like to be included in the photographs as you hand over the turkeys that they "earned" to the receiving organizations or individuals.

Thanksgiving will be here any minute, but there's enough time. Planning is as simple as writing down a one-page plan, calling the supermarket for a special co-sponsorship price, a few restaurants (for cooking), the press, and sending out a warm personal letter mailing to your customers and prospects.

Both the financial and the altruistic rewards will be significant, activity will grow and you will end up with a truly Happy New Year.

LESSON TWENTY-ONE

Marketing Is...

The point to all of this marketing talk. The times they are a changin'. How to keep up... or better yet, how to get ahead of the curve.

The *New York Times*, august national paper of record, has reported that high tech and the INTERNET are not eliminating travel. They're actually creating more of it.

The *Times* must consider this an important trend. In a medium where space is so tight that they count the quality of stories by column inches, this paper that created the phrase "all the news that's fit to print" has seen fit to give this story a whopping fifteen column FEET.

According to the story, "The gadgets that let business people fax, phone and surf the internet from 30,000 feet are

SMART MARKETING

the same technology that once promised to eliminate bothersome travel by heralding in a new age of video teleconferencing and the information superhighway with businessmen talking to each other by email and on television screens. Instead the opposite has happened...

"Futurists see increased travel as a sign of where business is heading - that face-to-face contact is becoming more important and the virtual office is making it easier to accomplish."

The *Times* draws the conclusion that the increasingly important face-to-face contact will not be accomplished through technology.

Well, that's wrong and I can prove it. Moreover, by studying market trends, which is what I preach best in these lessons and courses, I note that you can make money by earning while you learn how to cash in on the coming video conferencing growth industry, internet conferencing industry or any other paradigm shift...just by being a little bit ahead of the curve.

All modesty aside, it's amazing how right we have been over the last couple of years, just doubting obvious leaps of faith found in national newspapers. People who have agreed with our observations as to where the marketplace was REALLY taking us have made a modest bundle.

For instance, in 1993, when an analyst at then Kidder Peabody trashed Dell Computer in the *Wall Street Journal*, I disagreed with him in my computer column and predicted that Dell would come back within months. It did and many have laughed all the way to the bank.

And when IBM stock was hovering at around $46 per share, a top MBA from the renowned Gartner Group gave a speech, here in Stamford, CT, and predicted that IBM was finished. He cited at least a dozen practical reasons to short Big Blue's stock.

Lesson 21... Marketing IS . . .

When asked for my opinion, I told a business editor friend that IBM had a better than even money shot to double in two years. I guessed that money could be made by buying IBM stock, by selling IBM software, by becoming a strategic partner VAR with IBM, or all three.

Since then, it's come true. IBM's stock price has doubled and then doubled again. The company retains a commanding lead as one of the largest software companies in the world and IBM strategic partners have become a very happy lot.

But, enough about me. Let's get back to that *New York Times* article and how you can use news articles to improve your marketing presence. In this example, *The Times* concluded that the key deciding factors in how we communicate are:

1. The need to meet face-to-face.
2. The convenience of using technology to take our offices on the road.

I, on the other hand, concluded that the keys to communication are:
1. The ability to see the other person's facial expressions.
2. The checkbook.

In fact, the checkbook probably should be item number one since the checkbook has always ruled. If you cannot get a particular job done unless you are standing in front of the other guy or gal, the checkbook tells you that you need to be there to do business. Ergo, start packing.

On the other hand, if someone comes along who can show your boss how you can get the same job done "profitably" from your 8' by 8' Dilbert cell without racking up all those frequent-flier miles, well, friend, put back your expense vouchers, the checkbook says that your travelin' days are numbered.

SMART MARKETING ———

There will always be "road warriors", to be sure, but society, once again, is being segmented by technology and the checkbook. In the Army, we knew that it took six bodies in the rear to support one fighting man or woman at the front. Today in business, those six can stay put, back at the home office, or even office-at-home.

Some road warriors will, as the *Times* says, still spend 200 to 300 days on the road. But that won't be most of us. The majority of us will benefit from the face-to-face desktop interface that integrates your phone, your PC and you. Bill Gates thinks so, if you need more ammunition. Think. How often is Gates wrong in these matters?

Often, I find uses for videoconferencing. The turning point, for me, was the time I ran up the street to meet my friend Jules at our local MCI Worldcom sales office. Jules and I were involved with building a data network and internet access gateway to the big I-way for one of our clients using telecom services.

In the conference room with the account sales rep and the service specialist, we speakerphone-conference-called three people at the client site in Florida and an MCI engineer in Texas. The call took more than two and a half hours.

None of the locations were wired for video, nor data interchange, so, during the call we used a separate line to fax documents back and forth. We ironed out all of our technical issues and a few sales issues, but, I observed during the meeting that the use of videoconferencing would have improved communications and could have cut the meeting time in half...and it will when more locations are equipped.

At that time, I had a major client in the entertainment industry with two great communications expenses: phone and travel. After I told the CEO that we were going to save him a half million bucks a year on phone calls, he asked me how much

Lesson 21... Marketing IS...

of those savings would he have to reinvest for a videoconferencing system that would reduce his travel time and costs.

"Why do you want videoconferencing?" I asked.
"To see my managers eye-to-eye when they report to me." he answered. "I want to look 'em in the eyes to see what they're really thinking."
"Why don't you fly there?" I asked.
"Travel wastes too much time," He said. "If we can reduce travel time, then I can reduce my management staff by a third. That's a bigger expense than the airfare, hotels and car rentals."

This CEO was a forward thinker who ran an incredibly large company with the steep growth curve of a startup. Eventually, we tied in seven cities in three countries for him. His efficiency leaped forward and his costs went down even more.

A big reason is that the cost of videoconferencing has dropped to the canvas with the speed of a jaw that has just met the new Mike Tyson's clenched right fist. When Iron Mike went up the river the first time, most resellers couldn't build video for under $15,000 per site. Considering that you need at least as many people (sites) to video-conference as you do to tango, and sometimes as many as you need to conga, the checkbook issue kept us on airlines rather than phone lines.

But, by the day that Mike regained his freedom, the hardware costs had dropped to almost $3,000, with full motion picture quality, making it very affordable to start putting them in all over the place. Remember how few offices had fax machines when they cost more than $10k each? Now can you even find an office without two or three?

Communications peripherals have a way of becoming very ubiquitous when unit costs melt down. Those of us who are on the leading edge, while we are still few and far between, stand to make a systems integrating bundle, while saving our clients an even bigger one.

I began to recommend videoconferencing to our clients, just as I started to recommend integrating phone, voicemail, email and fax-back when they emerged as cost-effective productivity enhancements to business. Continuous speech recognizers, those that work,, will do the same thing for us, as will engines that convert the spoken word and handwritten text to computerspeak.

Regardless of the business you are in, you, too, can provide added value to what you sell, by making yourself aware of trends that common sense tells you are driven by your customer's checkbook. If you can identify those trends and you can integrate them into your value added products and services, don't just think about it... do it.

And stop worrying about the trends reported in the national press. They have the right research, but they get the conclusions all wrong. You are the guy, or gal, in the trenches and you have the experience to get it right.

Trust your own instincts, not just once, but over and over again. If there is any single lesson in marketing that you can profit from most, that is it. Finally, I'd like to suggest that you reread this course after a week, or two, and then drop me a line and let me know your thoughts. We will try to answer all correspondence and, if you have a suggestion for an upcoming edition, send it. If we use it, we will attribute it to you and we will send you a suitable gift.

When you are finished with this course, don't let it waste

Lesson 21... Marketing IS . . .

away on the shelf. Pass it along to a friend. We don't mind anyone getting a free ride. The more who benefit from this material, the happier we are.

Best of luck in your marketing efforts.

GIFT ORDER FORM (cut out and mail)

Make a list of the men and women you know who will thank you for decades to come for this simple act of kindness. Each book you order will be specially gift wrapped with a very tasteful card enclosed that says: *"I found this marketing course quite useful and thought you would like a copy. (Your name)."*

Save $8.20 per copy. Enclose your check in the amount of $29.95 for each gift-wrapped copy and we will waive the two-day, $3.20 postage, the $3.50 package cost and the $1.50 personalized greeting card. Or fill out and sign the MasterCard/Visa authorization (Connecticut residents must add 6% sales tax).

Number of books ordered: _____ Title(s): _____

Number times $29.95 each: _____

In CT add 6% tax: _____ Total enclosed, or charged: _____

MasterCard/Visa account: _____

Expiration date: _____

Name on card: _____

Signature: _____

Phone: _____ E-mail: _____

Show the gifts from: _____
(print clearly)

Send gifts to:

1. _____

2. _____

3. _____

For additional space, use other side, or photocopy.

For more than 10 copies, for corporate distribution, for quantity pricing and for on-site seminar information, call 1-203-323-6070, ext. 305, or click on http://www.smart-selling.com

✂ cut along this line — mail or fax to 203-356-1770

(Fold here. Tape 3 sides if including check)

Name: _____
Company: _____
Street: _____
City, State, ZIP: _____

Place Stamp Here

To:

Emery Publishing
800 Summer Street, Suite 340
Stamford, CT 06901

ORDER FORM (cut out and mail)

Book Title	Quantity	Cost/copy	Total
Smart Selling Twenty lessons that have helped thousands to earn millions. How you can turn ordinary selling into extraordinary income.	_____	$29.95	_____
Smart Marketing Marketing builds more revenue than selling alone and it's easy to do. Learn the secrets of brand building, public relations, and more, with scores of tips, tricks and lessons that produce immediate results.	_____	$29.95	_____
Smart Telemarketing Get more people to say "yes, yes" on the phone without ever meeting you in person.	_____	$9.00	_____

Connecticut orders, add 6% sales tax: _____

Total included with your order, or charged: _____

Coming soon
(check www.smart-selling.com for schedule)

Smart Management How you can use these powerful lessons of others to help you to build and lead a winning sales and management team. $29.95.

Smart Thinking Chicken soup may be good, but front line sales experience is better. How to use your own life experiences to reach success. $19.95.

Check enclosed: _____ Credit Card: _____

MasterCard/Visa account: _____

Expiration date: _____

Name on card: _____

Signature: _____

Your shipping address (no P.O. box for UPS)

Name: _____

Company: _____

Street address: _____

City: _____ ST: _____ ZIP: _____

Phone: _____ E-mail: _____

For more than 10 copies, for corporate distribution, for quantity pricing and for on-site seminar information call 1 (203) 323-6070, ext. 305, or click on http://www.smart-selling.com

(Fold here. Tape 3 sides if including check)

Name: _____
Company: _____
Street: _____
City, State, ZIP: _____

Place Stamp Here

To:

Emery Publishing
800 Summer Street, Suite 340
Stamford, CT 06901

READER RESPONSE FORM

(cut out and mail back. We will respond with a suitable token of appreciation.)

Dear Stan:

I have just finished this course, **Smart Marketing**, and I have the following questions, suggestions and/or comments to share with you for your next edition.

Your thoughts here (then fold the page in half and tape it, stamp it and mail it right back to us):

_____
_____
_____
_____
_____
_____
_____
_____
_____
_____
_____
_____
_____
_____
_____
_____
_____
_____

Phone: _____ E-mail: _____

cut along this line ✂ mail or fax to 203-356-1770

(Fold here. Tape 3 sides if including check)

Name: _____
Company: _____
Street: _____
City, State, ZIP: _____

Place Stamp Here

To:

Emery Publishing
800 Summer Street, Suite 340
Stamford, CT 06901